Praise for *Verdi's Shakespeare*

"Wills's insights into both Verdi's acute understanding of Shakespeare and his ingenious methods of conveying it are thrilling—particularly his account of how, when composing *Otello*, Verdi encapsulated the six hundred and eighty-six lines of the play's first act within a few minutes of music." —*The New Yorker*

"Wonderfully illuminating. This book is the product of a lifetime of listening and watching. . . . No lover of Verdi—or Shakespeare, for that matter—will want to miss it." —*Opera News*

"Riveting . . . a double-barreled salvo that hits two bull's-eyes. Shakespeare scholarship is one of the world's thriving industries, with no factories but worldwide workshops. While you are reading this, there must be hundreds (thousands?) of worthies turning out articles and books from pole to pole. But Garry Wills has upped the ante. There is a fair, but not daunting, amount of musical analysis, as well as much acknowledged borrowing and quoting from other relevant writers. This only makes the book more useful, what with burrowings (rather than borrowings) a worm would be proud of, and a panorama worthy of a fly's multifaceted eye. *Nomen est omen* goes a Latin adage: the name is a signifier. So the noun 'Wills' suggests manifold motivation, multiple resolve. Whatever Garry undertakes, trust Wills to get done." —John Simon, *The New York Times*

"Wills's joyously engaged, scholarly yet personable essay is not just a treat but also a banquet succulent enough to make Shakespeareans and Verdians of all who partake of it." —*Booklist* (starred review)

"Wills brilliantly explores the evolution, development, and performance histories of the three plays, the three operas, and the connections among them. An essential purchase." —*Library Journal* (starred review)

"Fascinating."   *—Commonweal Magazine*

"One genius interprets another: English to Italian, words to lyrics, immortal drama to overpowering opera. . . . While the book has an enormous amount to teach devotees of either Shakespeare or Verdi, opera fans in particular will enjoy the author's close and illuminating attention to backstage history, as well as words, music, and phrasing."   *—Kirkus Reviews*

"Throughout, [Wills] demonstrates an innate understanding of drama and music and how they can work together. His analyses of melody, harmony, and orchestration are as solid as his examination of theatrical practice and technique. And his research is thorough. He draws on the considerable store of data unearthed by others, citing in his more than one hundred footnotes a veritable Who's Who of opera and theater scholars."
                     —The Washington Independent Review of Books

PENGUIN BOOKS

VERDI'S SHAKESPEARE

Garry Wills has written many acclaimed and bestselling works, including *What Jesus Meant*, *Papal Sin*, and *Why I Am a Catholic*. His books have received many awards, including the Pulitzer Prize. His forthcoming work, *Why Priests?: The Real Meaning of the Eucharist*, will be published by Viking in 2013. A professor of history emeritus at Northwestern University, Wills is a frequent contributor to *The New York Review of Books* and other publications.

GARRY WILLS

Verdi's Shakespeare

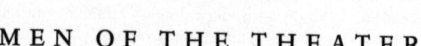

MEN OF THE THEATER

PENGUIN BOOKS

PENGUIN BOOKS

Published by the Penguin Group

Penguin Group (USA) Inc., 375 Hudson Street, New York, New York 10014, U.S.A.

Penguin Group (Canada), 90 Eglinton Avenue East, Suite 700, Toronto,
Ontario, Canada M4P 2Y3 (a division of Pearson Penguin Canada Inc.)

Penguin Books Ltd, 80 Strand, London WC2R 0RL, England

Penguin Ireland, 25 St. Stephen's Green, Dublin 2, Ireland (a division of Penguin Books Ltd)

Penguin Group (Australia), 707 Collins Street, Melbourne,
Victoria 3008, Australia (a division of Pearson Australia Group Pty Ltd)

Penguin Books India Pvt Ltd, 11 Community Centre,
Panchsheel Park, New Delhi–110 017, India

Penguin Group (NZ), 67 Apollo Drive, Rosedale, Auckland 0632,
New Zealand (a division of Pearson New Zealand Ltd)

Penguin Books, Rosebank Office Park, 181 Jan Smuts Avenue,
Parktown North 2193, South Africa

Penguin China, B7 Jaiming Center, 27 East Third Ring Road North,
Chaoyang District, Beijing 100020, China

Penguin Books Ltd, Registered Offices: 80 Strand, London WC2R 0RL, England

First published in the United States of America by Viking Penguin,
a member of Penguin Group (USA) Inc. 2011
Published in Penguin Books 2012

3 5 7 9 10 8 6 4 2

THE LIBRARY OF CONGRESS HAS CATALOGED THE HARDCOVER EDITION AS FOLLOWS:
Wills, Garry, 1934–
Verdi's Shakespeare : men of the theater / Garry Wills.
p. cm.
Includes bibliographical references and index.
ISBN 978-0-670-02304-2 (hc.)
ISBN 978-0-14-312222-7 (pbk.)
1. Shakespeare, William, 1564–1616—Adaptations—History and criticism. 2. Shakespeare, William,
1564–1616—Influence. 3. Verdi, Giuseppe, 1813–1901—Criticism and interpretation.
4. Verdi, Giuseppe, 1813–1901—Knowledge—Literature. 5. Opera—Italy—19th century. 6. Theater—
Italy—History—19th century. 7. Shakespeare, William, 1564–1616—Relations with actors.
8. Verdi, Giuseppe, 1813–1901—Relations with actors. I. Title.
PR2880.V4W56 2011
822.3'3—dc22   2011019768

Printed in the United States of America
Set in Dante MT Std   Designed by Francesca Belanger

To Barbara Gaines
director supreme

Contents

Contents

III. FALSTAFF

Key to Brief Citations

B   Julian Budden, *The Operas of Verdi,* three volumes (volume 1, Praeger Publishers, 1973; volumes 2 and 3, Oxford University Press, 1979, 1981).

C   E. K. Chambers, *The Elizabethan Stage,* four volumes (Clarendon Press, 1923).

F   Hans Busch, *Verdi's "Falstaff" in Letters and Contemporary Reviews* (Indiana University Press, 1997).

L   David Lawton, *Giuseppe Verdi "Macbeth,"* three volumes (University of Chicago Press, 2005).

M   David Rosen and Andrew Porter, *Verdi's "Macbeth": A Sourcebook* (Cambridge University Press, 1984).

O   Hans Busch, *Verdi's "Otello" and "Simon Boccanegra" in Letters and Documents,* two volumes paginated continuously (Clarendon Press, 1988).

INTRODUCTION
Comparative Dramaturgies

Verdi adored Shakespeare. Besides the three operas he took from him, he considered (though briefly) doing a *Tempest* or *Hamlet* or *Romeo and Juliet* (B 1.450). He considered for a very long time, and came near to creating, an opera from his favorite play, *King Lear*.[1] He did not take lightly the duty of being true to Shakespeare. When he read the score of Ambroise Thomas's *Hamlet,* he said of the librettists, "Poor Shakespeare! How they have mistreated him!" (B 2.711). He did not mean to mistreat the great dramatist himself. Hundreds of operas were derived from Shakespeare's plays—even more than from the works of Schiller, Goethe, or Walter Scott. Phyllis Hartnoll and her collaborators counted over 180 Shakespeare operas, but admitted they were missing some.[2] The editors of *The Oxford Companion to Shakespeare* claim the number is closer to 300.[3] Most of the operas in nineteenth-century Italy, France, and Germany were taken from the plays indirectly, from parallel sources, or from poor translations. Rossini's *Otello* (1816), for instance, was based on a French adaptation of Shakespeare's own Italian source, Cinthio's *Hecatommithi*. Bellini's *I Capuleti e i Montecchi* (1830) came from a play by Luigi Scevola.[4] Verdi was the first Italian composer who worked hard to get back to Shakespeare's authentic text.

Verdi could not read English—though his wife, who helped him, could—but he carefully compared the best recent translations (some made by his friends or acquaintances).[5] He had not been to England when he composed *Macbeth,* but he had acquired, from friends like Andrea Maffei, solid information on the way *Macbeth* was staged in the country of its origin (M 27). For *Macbeth,* he cut the play down to opera size himself, creating a prose synopsis for his librettist, Francesco Maria Piave, to versify. He was dissatisfied with Piave's work, correcting it, adding suggestions, above all trimming it. He wanted no waste words. He insisted to Piave, *"Poche parole! Poche parole! Poche parole!"* (Cut the words! Cut the words! Cut the words!) (M 10). Finally, in his exasperation with Piave, he had his scholar friend Andrea Maffei, an expert translator, correct portions of the libretto (M 69). Verdi worked himself so deeply into Shakespeare's mind that, in revising *Macbeth* for a Paris premiere, he took the gem of this performance—Lady Macbeth's aria "La luce langue"—directly from Shakespeare, in collaboration with his wife: "Verdi himself actually wrote the text for this aria—not only the detailed prose version he first sent to [his librettist] Piave on 15 December, but the verses themselves, to which the librettists made only a few minor changes" (L 1.xx).

Most of the many operas made from Shakespeare's plays are failures. Loose adaptations have been more successful—overtures, fantasias (like Tchaikovsky's *Romeo and Juliet*), incidental music (like Mendelssohn's for *A Midsummer Night's Dream*), variations (like Berlioz's *Beatrice and Benedict*). The rare success of a complete Shakespearean opera—like Benjamin Britten's *A Midsummer Night's Dream*—is a one-off for its composer. Verdi is the only composer who created three solid masterpieces from Shakespeare plays. They not only succeeded at the time of their premieres but have grown over the years, standing out even from Verdi's own impressive line of great works. The last two—*Otello* and *Falstaff*—are arguably the greatest things he ever wrote. He composed more operas from Schiller's plays (four) than from Shakespeare's, and some of the Schiller works are very impressive—especially *Don Carlos*. But none towers above his Shakespeare operas.

Verdi, across time and language barriers, obviously felt a great affinity with the dramatic ideals of his Elizabethan predecessor—and with good reason. The two men worked in theater conditions with many similarities. Both were supplying performances on a heavy schedule, to audiences with a voracious appetite for what they wrote. In a career of little over twenty years, Shakespeare turned out thirty-eight plays (along with some collaborations). Verdi had a longer career, of fifty-four years—but with a sixteen-year inactive period between *Aida* and *Otello*—in which he created twenty-seven operas (along with important revisions). These men were producing two major theatrical works a year during their most intense times, and were engaged in other poetic or musical compositions, as well as managerial and directorial work along the way. Shakespeare was composing narrative poems and sonnets. Verdi was composing religious and ceremonial and chamber music. Some of their contemporaries were even more prolific, especially Rossini in Verdi's young years.[6] The Elizabethan theaters were continually buzzing with new works, from dozens of aspiring playwrights, making the playhouses "pestiferous with plays" (as Bernard Shaw put it).[7] The pace of the professional life was unlike anything we see today, when a single play is kept in performance for long runs:

In the month of January, 1596 . . . the Admiral's Men played on every day except Sundays and presented fourteen plays.

Six were given only one performance in the month, and no play was presented more than four times. The shortest interval between the repetition of any single play was three days, and the next shortest five. Although all except one were old plays, this record represents an achievement that would almost certainly be beyond the capacities of actors in the modern theater.[8]

We can only be stunned at the memory powers of the actors on such a schedule. The opera houses of Verdi's time were just as bustling with new works and crowded seasons.

Shakespeare and Verdi were creative volcanoes. But mainly they were men of the theater, engaged in the companies they worked with, active at each stage of the production of the plays and operas that filled their lives, Shakespeare as an actor in his own and other men's plays, Verdi as a vocal coach and director of his works. Theirs was a hands-on life of the stage, not a remote life of the study.

Shakespeare

Those who doubt that Shakespeare wrote Shakespeare are working, usually, from a false and modern premise. They are thinking of the modern playwright, a full-time literary fellow who writes a drama and then tries to find people who will put it on—an agent to shop it around, a producer to put up the money, a theater as its venue, a director, actors, designers of sets and costumes, musicians and dancers if the play calls for them, and so on. Sometimes a successful playwright sets up an arrangement with a particular company (Eugene O'Neill and the Provincetown Players) or director (Tennessee Williams and Elia Kazan), but the process still begins with the writer creating his script, before elements are fitted around it, depending on things like which directors or actors are available for and desirous of doing the play. Producers complain that it is almost impossible to assemble the ideal cast for all the roles as the author envisioned them in his isolated act of creation. The modern writer owns the play by copyright and can publish it on his or her own, whether produced or not. None of these things was true of dramatic production in Shakespeare's time.

Then, the process began with the actors. They chose the playwright, not vice versa. They owned the play, to publish it or withhold it from publication. Each troupe had limited resources—often, nine to twelve adult actors (all male), and far fewer boy actors (sometimes as few as two). A Swiss traveler in 1599 saw "about fifteen" players handle the forty-five speaking parts in *Julius Caesar*.[9] An aspiring playwright had to bring his idea to these actors (or their representatives) with a plot accommodated to the number and talents of the particular troupe. The parts he was describing had to be arranged to allow for multiple doublings. A man playing two roles could not meet himself onstage, or even come back in as someone else too soon, to allow for costume and other changes (a beard, a wig, spectacles, padding, and so on). "For some thirty-five years, from 1547, plays advertise, usually on the title page, the number of actors required and how the parts may be doubled, trebled, and even septupled."[10] In a 1576 morality play, *The Tide Tarrieth No Man*, the Vice character is told to prolong his duel "while Wantonness maketh her ready" in the tiring house to come back out as Greediness.[11] The plot had to be tailored for the company from the very outset.

If the actors liked the concept of a play, they would normally recommend it to a theatrical entrepreneur (Philip Henslowe was the most famous of the half dozen or so working at the time) for an advance to the playwright while he finished the work. This advance was a loan, which the actors would pay back later, preferably from the proceeds of the play when performed. When the author finished writing his work, he read it to the company, which either accepted or rejected it at this point. If accepted, the script had to be presented to the Master of the Revels for state censorship, with payment for his reading it. He would often demand certain changes—or in some cases turn it down entirely. Only then, if cleared, could the play be put on. If, despite such screening, the play seemed seditious or libelous in the actual presentation, the actors were responsible along with the author and could be fined, suspended, jailed, even mutilated (by branding or ear cropping or nose cropping), or their theater could be closed.[12]

Thus, in the modern theater, performers are fitted to the play, but in Shakespeare's time, the play was fitted to the performers. If the playwright had an ongoing relationship with the troupe— like Shakespeare's with the Lord Chamberlain's Men (later the King's Men)—he could create his text for the known strengths of particular actors, as Shakespeare did for the talents of the great Richard Burbage, his principal resource. Shakespeare wrote comic scenes in different ways for the famous clown William Kemp and for the intellectual jester Robert Armin. He even took advantage of animal performers available to the cast. When the troupe had a trained dog, he wrote the part of Crab into *The Two Gentlemen of Verona*. When it had a young polar bear at hand, he wrote a scene stopper for *The Winter's Tale*: "Exit, pursued by a bear."[13] When he had two sets of players who looked alike, he wrote *The*

Comedy of Errors. In modern productions, with an established text, producers can shop around in a large pool of unattached actors to find two couples who are plausibly similar, but Shakespeare began with the four men already in his company and wrote the play to use them.

The trickiest job was to write for that rare commodity, the boy actors who played women. These were hard to come by and train in the brief time before their voices broke. That is why women's parts make up only 13 percent of the lines in Shakespeare's plays. The playwright had to know what stage of development each apprentice had reached. There were usually just two or three boys in the public plays (though more were available from choristers when a play was given at court or in a great family mansion). The boys' memories were such that Shakespeare wrote shorter parts for them than for adult actors—an average of 300 or so lines to the adults' 650 or so lines per play. But when he had a spectacular boy like John Rice, he was able to write as big a role for him as that of Cleopatra (693 lines).[14] Nothing could be more absurd than the idea of the Earl of Oxford writing a long woman's part without knowing whether the troupe had a boy capable of performing it.[15] Only Shakespeare, who knew and wrote for and acted with and coached John Rice, knew what he could do and how to pace him from play to play.

An acting company could not just pick up any boy off the street. The boy must have good voice and memory and diction—and preferably an ability to sing, dance, and perform on a musical instrument (like Lucius in *Julius Caesar*). When the Swiss traveler saw *Julius Caesar,* two of the adult actors and the play's only two boys came out and danced the after-show jig. Where to get such talented boys, and how to train them? Of course, there were all-boy theatrical troupes in the chapels and schools, very popular and with their own professional writers (C 1.23–76)—but some parents resented even those boys' playing in secular dramas.[16] The public theaters had much more trouble finding players for their female parts. Sometimes they could persuade a boy from the chapel or school to join them, or find a middle-class family with surplus boys willing to apprentice one—or even buy an apprentice from a troupe about to be dissolved. It was clearly hard finding and keeping boys with the requisite skills. (How many had to be dropped because the promise of talent proved illusory?)

Each boy had to be adopted as an apprentice, to live with an adult actor's family. The boys were given board, food, and training, but no wages. The adult master had to swear to the good morals of his charge in order to fend off Puritan attacks on the immorality of the theater. Shakespeare never had an apprentice of his own, since he did not have his family with him in London. John Rice was apprenticed to the manager of the company, John Hemings, who remembered him in his will (C 2.236). When any boy's apprenticeship ended, he could take advantage of his training by becoming a paid adult member of the troupe, or even a sharer in its property and profits. After marriage, he could acquire his own apprentice.

There are many signs of Shakespeare's crafting roles for particular boys. In three plays of the late 1590s, *A Midsummer Night's Dream, Much Ado About Nothing,* and *As You Like It,* he had one boy who was short and dark and another who was tall and fair. The contrast was so striking that Shakespeare made his lines play on it.[17] Shakespeare began with particular boys' talents, and then wrote his scenes around them. He must have had a boy from

Wales when he wrote *I Henry IV*, in which a woman speaks and sings Welsh. One of the experienced boys, in *As You Like It*, was good enough for Shakespeare to create his second-longest woman's role for him—Rosalind (686 lines). Very young apprentices were cast as little boys rather than as women, and they were given small parts to memorize—Macduff's son in *Macbeth* (21 lines), Lucius in *Julius Caesar* (34 lines), Prince Edward in *Richard III* (51 lines), and so on. As they matured in age and training, Shakespeare could give them larger roles as boys, like that of Prince Arthur in *King John* (120 lines) or the clever Moth in *Love's Labor's Lost* (116 lines). Only as they advanced further into their teens could he trust them with important women's roles, and with the doubling made necessary by the small number of boys for female roles. A boy recruited at age eleven or twelve had perhaps five years of training and performance before him.

Such experienced boys, a rare resource, had to be used with great economy. Lady Macbeth, as important as she is, has only one brief appearance (20 lines) in the last two acts of the play. That is because John Rice was needed to double Lady Macduff (45 lines) in Act 3. It is poignant that Lady Macbeth, who was not in on the murder of Macduff's wife, somehow learned of it before the sleepwalking scene, when she sings a folk song, as many mad characters do in Shakespeare: "The Thane of Fife [Macduff] had a wife—where is she now?" (5.1.42–43). Cordelia in *King Lear* is absent from the play for an even longer time than Lady Macbeth. After the play's first scene (41 lines), Cordelia is gone from the rest of Act 1 and all of Acts 2 and 3. She shows up in the last two acts to speak only 48 lines. This seems a very uneconomical use of a trained boy, until we notice that Cordelia exits the first scene well before the Fool shows up, and the Fool disappears before

Cordelia returns. The Fool is an innocent "natural," sexless and accidentally wise, unlike the "allowed fools" played by Robert Armin (Feste, Touchstone). Armin, it seems, played the "mad" Edgar, while a boy doubled Cordelia and the Fool.[18]

Shakespeare was not a full-time writer without other responsibilities, like O'Neill or Williams. But what might look like a distraction for such authors—acting in his own and other people's plays, coaching fellow players, helping manage the ownership of the troupe's resources (including its two theaters, the Globe and Blackfriars)—was a strength for Shakespeare, since it made him a day-by-day observer of what the troupe could accomplish, actor by actor. The company was, after all, mounting plays with bewildering rapidity, studying, memorizing, and rehearsing in the morning and evening while performing in the afternoon. Without that experience, Shakespeare could not have written as he did. William Ringler observed how Shakespeare wrote to and for the individual actors on his team:

> It is fascinating to observe step by step the skillful generalship with which Shakespeare marshals his characters, observes the convention of scene breaks, and arranges the entrances and exits of characters in one scene so that those needed in the following scene are available for their parts, and where doubling is required have adequate time for changes of costume and makeup. . . . Analysis of the casting reveals that he usually kept remarkably accurate track of the personnel of his company. . . . Scenes opening with a large number of characters are always preceded by scenes or ends of scenes with only a few characters, so that adequate time is allowed for the shifting around of the small cast and for doubling. . . . Shakespeare himself was careful to distribute the number of lines among

the members of his cast according to their capacities. . . . Shakespeare usually constructed his plays very tightly and made maximum use of all the actors available to him.[19]

Sir Francis Bacon or the Earl of Oxford, writing at home, could not have known such things. As Ivor Brown says, "Shakespeare was as much on and around a stage as in his study."[20]

Shakespeare could not publish his plays. He did not own them—the troupe did, and it published them only after Shakespeare's death, when keeping a monopoly on them for performance was a less pressing matter. (Most Shakespeare quartos were unauthorized by the company.) And Shakespeare could not write just anything he wanted. The company had to agree that it was a commercially viable project. Furthermore, sharers in the troupe could change things, ask for cuts or rewriting, add things on their own, or tell Shakespeare to add them—as happened with Thomas Middleton's new Hecate songs for *Macbeth*. When the company had at a court performance more boys to play witches, Middleton wrote them in.

All this is far from the picture of Shakespeare in action that was provided by Edward Dowden's once-influential book, *Shakspere: A Critical Study of His Mind and Art* (1875), which made Shakespeare's work reflect a psychomachia of the playwright's spiritual development. The plays, Dowden argued, fall into four periods, each reflecting a different stage in Shakespeare's inner life. Dowden called the four eras

> In the Workshop
> In the World
> Out of the Depths
> On the Heights.[21]

By this standard Shakespeare's inner serenity later in life made him write the romances. But a look at what other playwrights were doing at the same time shows that romances had become a popular genre and the company wanted its part in that market. Actually, if a life cycle of maturing is suggested in the course of the plays, it would apply not to Shakespeare but to Richard Burbage. His is the youthful ardor of Romeo, the warrior heroism of Henry V, "the sere, the yellow leaf" of Macbeth, the "vale of years" of Othello, the wisdom of Prospero watching a younger generation of lovers.

Shakespeare made Burbage an even greater celebrity than Edward Alleyn, Marlowe's star player. When contemporaries remembered Hamlet, they did not think Shakespeare, they thought Burbage. Richard Burbage went from his twenties to his forties continually playing in the Shakespeare repertory (along with the work of other authors, like Ben Jonson). He was the principal factor in the success of the Lord Chamberlain's/King's Men, the most stable and prosperous theater company of Elizabethan and Jacobean times. Its sharers were especially loyal to each other, as one can tell from the regular way they left grants in their wills to colleagues and former boy apprentices. Only one sharer left the company, the star comic Will Kemp, who departed in 1599 to begin his spectacular dancing tour of the country. The others remained, and they became a great tuned human instrument Shakespeare played on with constantly varying skill.

⟨ Verdi

The working methods of a composer of operas in the nineteenth century had much in common with those of an Elizabethan playwright—enough to make them ideal subjects for a study in comparative dramaturgies. The playwright had to tailor his drama to the resources of a particular acting company. The composer had to fit his music to the voices available to him in a particular opera house. Rossini, in his long association with the Naples theater, the San Carlo, had to give most male parts to tenors, since that was where the troupe was strongest. In his version of *Othello,* the Moor is a tenor, Iago is a tenor, Rodrigo is a tenor, the Doge is a tenor, and the gondolier is a tenor. Only Desdemona's father, not a very important role, is a bass.[22] Among the women singers, Rossini had to compose with the skills of Isabella Colbran in mind, since she was the house star (and she would be his mistress, later his wife).

When Verdi did his version of *Macbeth,* he had only one weak tenor at hand, and he gave him the minor role of Macduff, with only one aria late in the opera. He did not let him sing his own climax-song (cabaletta) alone, but had the chorus join in with him (L 1.xvi). He had chosen *Macbeth* as a subject because he knew he could get by with only a minor contribution from the tenor, so long as he had a great baritone—which he demanded from the theater—to play Macbeth. When he received at first his commission for an opera at the Teatro della Pergola in Florence, he was initially undecided over setting Schiller's *Die Räuber* or *Macbeth.* For the Schiller he would need a good tenor, and the manager said the house could not get the one Verdi had in mind (Gaetano Fraschini). So it had to be *Macbeth.* In modern performance, it is hard to get a star tenor to sit out the night waiting for his one aria. Only in the recording studio will a Pavarotti or Domingo come in for the chance to sing "Ah, la paterna mano." When the opera was put on in Paris, the impresario defied Verdi's express ban and expanded the tenor role, giving him an extra cabaletta and letting him repeat Lady Macbeth's drinking song (L 1.xxix).

Even with a proven performer like Felice Varesi singing the role of Macbeth, Verdi was tailoring and adjusting the part as he composed—he gave Varesi three differently scored versions of his final scene, asking him which he thought would fit his voice better (B 1.4). When he sent her first music to his Lady Macbeth (Marianna Barbieri-Nini), he wrote, "If there should be some passage that lies badly [for your voice], let me know before I do the orchestration [for the passage that needs change]" (M 30). He did the same with Varesi, writing him: "I'm convinced that the tessitura [range] suits you well, but there could be some notes or passages that are uncomfortable for you, so write to me before I orchestrate it" (M 36). He asked Barbieri about the state of her trill before writing trills into her role (M 29)—after her assurances, he gave her many trills in her drinking song. Just as it would make no sense for Shakespeare to write a Cleopatra if he did not know John Rice's ability, it would make no sense to write trills for a part unless Verdi knew he had a singer capable of them. When Barbieri objected to the idea of reading without music the letter from Macbeth, Verdi said he would set it to music if she preferred that (M 40).

This was typical of the tailoring to specific voices that was demanded of the opera composer. He, like Shakespeare, had to be a man of the stage. He was expected to coach the singers and direct the first performances of his work. "According to Pacini, it was the custom at the San Carlo theater, Naples, for the composer to turn the pages for the leading cello and double bass players on opening nights" (B 1.5). The composer had to change his score to fit new voices if there were substitutions caused by illness or some accident. In subsequent performances, he was expected to take out or put in arias for the different houses, transposing keys and changing orchestration. He was a man not of the study but of the theater.

This hands-on approach to composition had long been the case. As Julian Budden writes:

> In the eighteenth century . . . the singer, not the composer, was the starting-point. When Mozart was a youth no one would dream of composing an aria until he had first heard the artist who was to perform it, and this might be no more than a fortnight before the premiere. Thus, for instance, Leopold Mozart to his wife during the composition of *Mitridate, Re di Ponto* in Milan in 1770: "Wolfgang has composed only one aria for the *primo uomo,* since he has not yet arrived and Wolfgang doesn't want to do the same work twice over." More than sixty years later, when Bellini was writing *I Puritani* for the Théâtre des Italiens in Paris, the situation was no different. "The whole of the first act is now finished, except for the trio, because I want first to try it out (*provarlo*) on [the tenor] Rubini." *Provare* is the word used for trying on a suit. Bellini's contemporary, Giovanni Pacini, one of the most prolific operatic practitioners of his day, wrote in his memoirs that he always tried to serve his singers as a good tailor serves his clients, "concealing the natural defects of the figure and emphasizing the good points." (B 1.3–4)

Early in the nineteenth century, temperamental sopranos (or those sleeping with the theater manager) could just ignore the score if they did not like it and put in a favorite aria from another work—what were called "trunk arias" (*arie di baule*), since the singer carried around scores to be inserted at her whim. As

Budden says, "It was only in England that Handel was able to hold a prima donna out of the window until she complied with his wishes" (B 1.4). Handel was escaping what Budden wryly calls "the tyranny of good voices" (B 1.6). Some composers kept a singer from using other men's work by yielding to the performer's wish for a special aria from the maestro himself: "Verdi wrote a new tenor cabaletta for *I Due Foscari* and a new cavatina for *Giovanna d'Arco* to oblige the singers Mario and Sofia Loewe respectively" (B 1.5). In fact, Verdi regularly composed substitute arias for a singer in his first seven operas—abandoning the practice only as his prestige grew.[23] Verdi was able to gain greater creative control over his work as his career developed. Later on, he could threaten a manager that he would withdraw his work from performance, even after the last rehearsal, if he did not get the performers, the rehearsal time, the direction and costumes and lighting he wanted.

In this book, I shall therefore begin the treatment of each play or opera with the performers the author/composer had in mind. We have to rely on guesswork for much of Shakespeare's troupe, since there are no cast lists for Shakespeare's plays (as opposed to Ben Jonson's). But we know what type of player he used, and the demands (like doubling) he had to allow for. He always had Burbage, of course. He did not want to overwork him—he gave him a comparatively short role (Julius Caesar) between two demanding long ones (Henry V, Hamlet)—but he always wanted him onstage, since he was the company's principal draw.[24]

We are fortunate in having the names and histories of the singers Verdi dealt with, and we can trace his worries, frustrations, and satisfactions with them in his ample correspondence, conveniently collected by David Rosen and Andrew Porter for *Macbeth* and by Hans Busch for *Otello* and *Falstaff*.

There are other similarities between the conditions of Shakespeare and of Verdi, besides their writing for particular performers. Both had to put up with a demanding and prior censorship from the political authorities. Verdi's problems were greater than Shakespeare's. The British companies had to deal only with the state machinery of Queen Elizabeth or King James. But since Italy was divided into various political jurisdictions—papal, Austrian, Neapolitan, Florentine—and each jurisdiction had competing authorities overseeing morals, the approval process was a marathon of trials. What was approved in one place could be rejected when the work was taken to another city's opera house. This was not just a matter of minor changes. Often the whole libretto had to be rewritten in order to be politically acceptable. The time of the story, the locale, the characters, had all to be changed. In papal Rome alone, these kinds of changes were required:

> Verdi's *Giovanna d'Arco* became *Orietta di Lesbo*, Rossini's *Guillaume Tell* became *Rodolfo di Stirling*. Throughout Italy, after the failure of the war of independence in 1848–9, *La Battaglia di Legnano* became *L'Assedio d'Arlem*; *Le Roi s'amuse* was eventually rendered respectable by being transformed into *Rigoletto*.[25]

When Verdi planned an opera on the adultery of Gustav III of Sweden, he was first compelled to change the story to avoid the assassination of a Swedish monarch. For performance in Naples, the opera became the tale of a Pomeranian duke, *A Masked Revenge (Una Vendetta in Domino)*. But any European assassination was considered unacceptable, and the opera finally appeared in

Rome as *A Masked Ball (Un Ballo in Maschera)*, the story of a colonial governor of Boston—though, as Philip Gossett says, "To place *Ballo* in Boston is like setting *Traviata* in Munich."[26] Outside Rome, what was *Stiffelio* in Trieste, the story of a Protestant minister with an adulterous wife, became *Aroldo* in Rimini, the story of an English crusader (B 2.337). *Les Vêpres Siciliennes* was changed for Naples to *Batilda di Turenne* (B 2.369).

Another resemblance between the theater of Shakespeare and that of nineteenth-century opera is the crossing of gender lines. The Puritans had kept women off the stage in England, and the papacy kept women from choirs in Rome. Boys had to play the roles in England, castrated men in Italy. Though the use of castrati was disappearing in the nineteenth century, it was suggested that the brilliant boy soprano Gioacchino Rossini should become one.[27] The castrato tradition shifted into the "pants roles" of male parts sung by women—like Rossini's Tancredi, Donizetti's Smeton, or Meyerbeer's Urbain. Verdi has few women sing as boys, but there is Oscar of *Ballo in Maschera* and the boy apparitions of *Macbeth*. He also planned to make the Fool in his version of *King Lear* a woman (B 1.7).

All in all, the blend of illusion and professionalism, of artifice and heightened reality, of soaring poetry and melodic ambition, makes the theater of Shakespeare and that of Verdi similar in many ways, obvious and hidden. I mean to explore those ways here.

Notes

1. On Verdi's long engagement with *King Lear,* see Philip Gossett, "The Hot and Cold Verdi Writes to Antonio Somma about *Re Lear*," in *Variations on the Canon,* edited by Robert Curry et al. (University of Rochester Press, 2008).

2. Phyllis Hartnoll, *Shakespeare in Music* (Macmillan, 1964), pp. 26–82. Hartnoll and her collaborators list thirty-two operas from *The Tempest*, twenty-four from *Romeo and Juliet*, fourteen from *Hamlet*.

3. Michael Dobson and Stanley Wells, *The Oxford Companion to Shakespeare*, corrected edition (Oxford University Press, 2008), pp. 325–28. Though they find some full operas not listed by Hartnoll, they include English Restoration versions of the plays with musical additions.

4. The Romeo and Juliet theme was set to music by Marescalchi (1785), Zingarelli (1796), Guglielmi (1810), Vaccai (1825), and Torriani (1828). But no opera was based directly on Shakespeare's play until Marchetti's in 1865.

5. William Weaver argues that Verdi used and compared six translations of *Macbeth* in collaborating on the libretto of his opera (M 144–48).

6. Rossini in twenty years wrote forty operas. For the Elizabethan theater, Thomas Heywood wrote, alone or in various collaborations, 220 plays, Thomas Dekker wrote 64, Philip Massinger 55. See Gerald Eades Bentley, *The Profession of Dramatist in Shakespeare's Time, 1590–1642* (Princeton University Press, 1971), pp. 27–28.

7. George Bernard Shaw, review of *Macbeth* in the *Saturday Review*, May 25, 1883.

8. David Bradley, *From Text to Performance in the Elizabethan Theatre* (Cambridge University Press, 1992), p. 33.

9. Thomas Platter, quoted at C 2.365.

10. F. P. Wilson, *The English Drama, 1485–1585* (Oxford University Press, 1969), p. 49.

11. Ibid., p. 65.

12. For the mode of putting on plays in Shakespeare's time, see the detailed and amply documented accounts in Bentley, op. cit., and Gerald Eades Bentley, *The Profession of Player in Shakespeare's Time, 1590–1642* (Princeton University Press, 1984). Also C 1.71–105, 348–88, and Neil Carson, *A Companion to Henslowe's Diary* (Cambridge University Press, 1988), pp. 67–79.

13. It used to be thought that the "bear" was a man in a costume. But scholars have now focused on the fact that two polar bear cubs were brought back from the waters off Greenland in 1609, that they were turned over to Philip Henslowe's bear collection (hard by the Globe Theatre), and that polar bears show up in three productions of the 1610–11 theatrical season—the old play *Mucedorus*, revived in 1610 with

added scenes for the bear, Ben Jonson's 1611 masque *Oberon*, with a bear-drawn chariot, and *The Winter's Tale* (1610–11). Polar bears become fierce at pubescence and were relegated to bear baiting, but the cubs were apparently still trainable in their young state. Since polar bears are such good swimmers, the king even turned them loose in the Thames to have aquatic bear baitings. See Barbara Ravelhofer, "'Beasts of Recreacion': Henslowe's White Bears," *ELR* 32 (2002), pp. 287–323, and Teresa Grant, "Polar Performances: The King's Bear Cubs on the Jacobean Stage," *Times Literary Supplement*, June 14, 2002.

14. For more about John Rice, see chapter 1.

15. The numbers of lines per character I take from T. J. King, *Casting Shakespeare's Plays: London Actors and Their Roles, 1590–1642* (Cambridge University Press, 1992). Different counts are arrived at according to the way lines are assigned to prose speeches.

16. See the complaint of Henry Clifton at his son's being pressed into being a player for the Children of the Chapel (Bentley, *Profession of Player*, pp. 47–48).

17. *Midsummer*, 3.2.257, 263, 274, 290–326, 343; *As You Like*, 1.3.115, 3.2.269; *Much Ado*, 1.1.173, 214.

18. See Richard Abrams, "The Double Casting of Cordelia and Lear's Fool," *Texas Studies in Literature and Language* 27 (1987), pp. 354–68, and Skiles Howard, "Attendants and Others in Shakespeare's Margins: Doubling in the Two Texts of *King Lear*," *Theatre Survey* 32 (1991), pp. 187–213. In considering that a boy played Fool, we should remember that Verdi wanted a woman to play Fool in his planned *Re Lear*, and the best Fool I ever saw was Emma Thompson in a Chicago production early in her career. She played the role hunched over to look small and speaking in a singsong falsetto. When at the curtain call she straightened up into her full height and beauty, there was an appreciative gasp in the house.

19. William A. Ringler, Jr., "The Number of Actors in Shakespeare's Early Plays," in Gerald Eades Bentley, ed., *The Seventeenth Century Stage: A Collection of Critical Essays* (University of Chicago Press, 1968), pp. 115–21.

20. Ivor Brown, *Shakespeare and the Actors* (Coward-McCann, 1970), p. 65.

21. See S. Schoenbaum, *Shakespeare's Lives*, new edition (Oxford University Press, 1991), p. 359: "No biographical pattern imposed on Shakespeare

before or since has made as profound an impact as Dowden's. The Dublin professor is the only academic critic of Shakespeare whose work would remain uninterruptedly in print for almost a century."

22. Philip Gossett tells me that the French, when they ruled Naples, banned both castrati and the mezzo-sopranos who had performed high male roles, leaving the field to tenors.

23. Hilary Poriss, *Changing the Score: Arias, Prima Donnas, and the Authority of Performance* (Oxford University Press, 2009), pp. 23–24.

24. For casting Burbage as Caesar, see Wills, *Rome and Rhetoric* (Yale University Press, 2011).

25. David R. B. Kimbell, *Verdi in the Age of Italian Romanticism* (Cambridge University Press, 1981), p. 27.

26. Philip Gossett, *Scholars and Divas: Performing Italian Opera* (University of Chicago Press, 2006), p. 496.

27. Herbert Weinstock, *Rossini* (Alfred A. Knopf, 1968), pp. 14–15.

I

Macbeth

I

Macbeth's First Performers

❧ Shakespeare's Actors

RICHARD BURBAGE AND JOHN RICE

The first Lady Macbeth was, by all the laws of probability, the star boy actor of the 1606–7 season, John Rice. On 16 July 1607, Rice was given a prominent role when the Merchant Taylors' Company entertained King James I at its guildhall in London. Rice was dressed beautifully as an angel of light bearing a taper of frankincense, and he delivered an eighteen-line speech specially composed for the occasion by Ben Jonson. For this service, the Taylors' Company records the following payments: "To Mr. Hemings [Rice's master in the acting troupe] for his direction of his boy that made the speech to His Majesty, 40 shillings, and five shillings given to John Rice, the speaker" (C 2.213).

In 1610, in a Thames-side water pageant to honor the investiture of the Prince of Wales, Burbage and Rice played a little drama written by Anthony Munday, appearing as the water royalties, Amphion and Corinea (C 2.336). The state disbursement records recall the occasion:

> It is ordered that Mr. Chamberlain shall pay unto Mr. Burbage and John Rice, the players that rode upon the two fishes and made the speeches at the meeting of the high and mighty prince the Prince of Wales upon the River of

Thames on Thursday last, seventeen pounds, ten shillings, and six pence, by them disbursed for robes and other furniture for adorning themselves at the same meeting. And that they shall retain to their own use, in lieu of their pains there taken, such taffeta, silk and other necessaries as were provided for that purpose, without any further allowance.[1]

That this ceremony made a spectacular mark is clear from contemporary accounts, calling Burbage and Rice

two absolute actors, even the very best our instant time can yield. . . . [Burbage as] Amphion the Father of Harmony or Music . . . a grave and judicious prophetlike personage, attired in his apt habits every way answerable to his state and profession, with his wreath of sea shells on his head and his harp hanging in fair twine before him . . . [Rice] a very fair and beautiful nymph representing the genius of old Corineus' queen and the province of Cornwall's, suited in her watery habit yet rich and costly, with a coronet of pearls and cockle shells on her head.[2]

Given the now-accepted date for *Antony and Cleopatra,* 1606— a year before Rice was a beautiful angel of light at the Taylors' Company and three years before he was a fair and beautiful nymph at the Thames pageant—it is clear that Shakespeare gave the long and difficult role of Cleopatra to this "absolute" actor. This means that Rice played the role in the spectacular Christmas–Candlemas season at court, where the King's Men gave eight plays at the peak of the company's power and fame. Documents give the dates of these performances, but name only two of them (C 4.121–22). Here is the calendar:

December 26, *King Lear*
December 29
January 4
January 8
February 2, *The Devil's Charter* (by Barnabe Barnes)
February 5
February 15
February 27

Two of the plays performed in the blank dates were *Macbeth* and *Antony and Cleopatra*. *Macbeth* could well have been performed in the position just before or just after *The Devil's Charter*, since (as we shall see) the two plays make a diabolic pair.

In fact, witchcraft is a theme of at least three of the plays, and it seems likely that Rice was the beautiful witch in all three.[3] Cleopatra is often called a witch in her play. Pompey says of her, "Let witchcraft join with beauty, lust with both" (2.1.22). Antony is called "The noble ruin of her magic" (3.10.18). When Antony's fleet is deserted by Cleopatra, he refers to her as "this grave charm" and shouts, "Ah, thou spell!" and uses the apotropaic guard against witches, "Avaunt!" (4.12.25, 30). He even says of her, "The witch shall die" (4.12.47). It was believed that witches suckled their animal familiars from their devil spot, an image that comes to mind when Cleopatra refers to the asp that bites her:

Dost thou not see my baby at my breast,
That sucks the nurse asleep? (5.2.309–10)

In *The Devil's Charter*, Barnes tells the story of the wicked pope Alexander VI, and his children Cesare Borgia and Lucrezia

Borgia (in Barnes's English, Caesar and Lucretia). The devil rises from hell to put the papal tiara on Alexander. Lucretia commits incest with her papal father and her cardinal brother, and stabs her husband. She is far more murderous than Lady Macbeth. Both characters are, by the laws of the time, criminal witches. Lady Macbeth summons diabolical instruments to give her unnatural power. She has a "familiar" spirit, the raven (1.5.38)—probably the same familiar ("Harpier") that belongs to the third witch (4.1.3).

> Come, you spirits
> That tend on mortal thoughts, unsex me here,
> And fill me from the crown to the toe topful
> Of direst cruelty! Make thick my blood,
> Stop up th' access and passage to remorse,
> That no compunctious visitings of nature
> Shake my fell purpose, nor keep peace between
> Th' effect and it! Come to my woman's breasts,
> And take my milk for gall, you murth'ring ministers,
> Wherever in your sightless substances
> You wait on nature's mischief! (1.5.40–50)

Barnes's Lucretia makes a similar invocation to the evil spirits, to aid her as she prepares to murder her husband:

> You grisly Daughters of grim Erebus,
> Which spit out vengeance from your viperous hairs,
> Infuse a three-fold vigor in these arms,
> Immarble more my strong indurate heart,
> To consummate the plot of my revenge. (1.5.572–77)

John Rice must at times have had to remind himself which witch was saying which evil words, Lady Macbeth or Lucretia.

In an odd historical footnote, the brilliant boy actor who played these evil women, these traffickers with devils, retired from the stage after serving as an adult member of the troupe, and became—a *clergyman*. The actor who had looked like an angel as a boy became a heavenly minister. Hemings, his former master in the company, left twenty shillings in his will to "John Rice, clerk of St. Saviour's in Southwark" (C 2.336). Rice is included in the "principal actors" of Shakespeare's works, as listed in the First Folio. He was surely one of the most important actors in Shakespeare's troupe, a regular partner to Burbage himself, and the first Lady Macbeth.

Burbage and Rice were clearly an impressive pair, not only in the two royal entertainments for which they were specially appointed in this period but in the stunning Christmas season of 1606–7, when Burbage was Lear to Rice's Fool/Cordelia, and Macbeth to Rice's Lady, and Alexander VI to Rice's Lucretia. Shakespeare knew how to use two such brilliant players when he had them together.

In *Macbeth*, Rice spoke only a third as many lines as Burbage, and almost all of them are in the first two acts, when the murder is conceived and carried out. After that, the characters shrink into their lonely isolation. Macbeth does not see his wife's illness or sleepwalking or death. She dies alone, after living alone. There is a reverse dynamic between them. In the first two acts, she is the driving force while he hesitates or balks. But after he takes charge, he cuts her out of his plans: "Be innocent of the knowledge, dearest chuck" (3.2.45). It is often said that we do not witness her deterioration from the commanding figure of the opening scenes. Only after she has been broken do we see her sleepwalk in her brief last scene (twenty lines). We are given some early hints of vulnerability. She says, "I have given suck, and know / How tender 'tis to love the babe that milks me" (1.7.54–55), and she cannot kill Duncan in his sleep because he looks like her father (2.2.12–13). She faints when the murder is revealed.

One of the signs of what is going on inside her is the scene in which Macduff's wife and child are killed. Lady Macbeth betrays her knowledge of Lady Macduff's murder when she sings in her sleep, "The Thane of Fife had a wife; where is she now?" (5.1.42–43). John Rice played Lady Macduff, and the implications of that murder must register with an audience that knows Rice is enacting a scene with emotional resonance for the woman who has given suck and knows what 'tis to love the babe that milks her. Doubling can deepen the meaning of both roles being played—as when Rice played both Cordelia and the Fool, those who love Lear while he mistreats them. The emotional breakdown of Lady Macbeth is signaled in the murder of Lady Macduff.

⸙ Verdi's Singers

Felice Varesi and Marianna Barbieri-Nini

Verdi tailored his opera to specific voices, just as Shakespeare had shaped his heroes and heroines to Burbage and Rice. At this point in his career, Verdi was determined to break away from "the tyranny of good singing," from the empty beauties of bel canto. He was aiming for something grittier, closer to the dark and even grotesque tale Shakespeare had given him. He called the story "gothic"—*fantastico* is his word for the grotesqueries loved by the Romantic Period. He wanted human beings whom the witches have literally infected with evil. He went so far as to say not only that the characters' singing should be ugly but that they should themselves *look* ugly, like medieval symbols of vice. The bad looks that were held against the two singers he chose were, for him, an advantage. When the opera went to Naples in 1848, the impresario wanted to cast the beautiful soprano Eugenia Tadolini as Lady Macbeth. Verdi resisted emphatically:

> You know how highly I regard Tadolini, and she herself knows it; but I believe it's necessary—for the interest of all concerned—to make a few observations to you.[4] Tadolini's qualities are far too good for that role. This may perhaps seem absurd to you. . . . Tadolini has a beautiful and attractive appearance, and I would like Lady to be ugly and evil. Tadolini sings to perfection, and I would like Lady not to sing. Tadolini has a stupendous voice, clear, limpid, powerful, and I would like Lady to have a harsh, stifled, and hollow (*cupa*) voice. Tadolini's voice has an angelic quality. I would like Lady's voice to have a diabolical quality. (M 66–67)

Verdi did not get the first soprano he wanted in 1847—Sofia Loewe, who had sung in the premieres of Verdi's *Ernani* and *Attila*. She withdrew from contention for Lady Macbeth to have an abortion (L 1.xii). As it turned out, Verdi was happy to get Marianna Barbieri-Nini for the role, not least because of her striking bad looks. In 1851, when she sang as Donizetti's Lucrezia

Borgia in London, the famous music critic Henry Chorley wrote of her:

> Unsightly is a gentle adjective as applied in her case. There is an expressive ugliness which can be turned to a certain account on the stage—an unmarked meanness of feature which genius can light up and animate, but Madame Barbieri-Nini's uncomeliness was at once large and mean, a thing to be escaped from, and unvarying. (M 14)

Verdi knew what Barbieri-Nini was capable of—she had sung in his *I Due Foscari*—and he did not want a beautiful woman striking beautiful poses as his Lady Macbeth.

He set the same seemingly perverse standard for his baritone protagonist, Felice Varesi:

> Varesi is the only artist in Italy today who is able to do the part I have in mind, both because of his style of singing and his feeling—and even because of his appearance. All other artists, even those better than he, could not do that part for me as I'd like—not to detract from the merits of [Gaetano] Ferri, who is better looking, has a more beautiful voice, and, if you like, is even a better singer, but in that role certainly couldn't give me the effect that Varesi would. (M 5)[5]

Though Varesi was not as startling in appearance as Barbieri, Verdi's close assistant, the conductor Emanuele Muzio, did not hesitate to call him, too, "ugly" (M 7). He was small and unimposing, despite his great voice. Verdi would give him his signature role as the hunchbacked Rigoletto in 1851, four years after

Macbeth. The composer wanted the suggestion of a distorted soul in his Macbetto.[6]

Verdi always labored intensely over the words of his operas, issuing endless demands to his librettists, wanting the accents to fall just right for the singing. He chose and corrected the poetic meters being used, and quibbled to find exactly the right word for each situation. Then he coached the singers to make sure they made the words clear and understandable out in the house. In the case of *Macbeth*, his own reverence for Shakespeare made him even more obsessive about the libretto. He rehearsed the singers for hours. Barbieri clearly exaggerates when she says he went over her duet with Varesi 150 times, but Verdi's letters show how insistent he was on the precise delivery he desired. He said he wanted the lines to seem more spoken than sung (L 1.xvi). He told both principal singers, "I want the performer to serve the poet better than they serve the composer" (M 29, 30). He went so far as to say that his singers *should not sing*.

He was creating a new kind of opera. Barbieri expected to perform an entry aria (cavatina), which is why she objected to the idea of appearing reading a letter without any musical notes at all (M 39). Varesi expected his own cavatina, but Verdi said he must first be caught in dialogue with Banco (M 30), a very Shakespearean procedure. Verdi wanted the words to leap out at the audience, unfiltered by bel canto filigrees. He worked especially on Lady Macbeth's sleepwalking scene, which was for him the climax of the opera. Barbieri recalled:

> I tried to imitate those who talk in their sleep, uttering words (as Verdi would say to me) while hardly moving their

lips, leaving the rest of the face immobile, including the eyes. It was enough to drive me crazy. (M 51)[7]

If anyone doubts that the singer can speak through the music, he or she should listen to Maria Callas performing the sleepwalking scene in her 1952 La Scala live recording. Her first words, *"Una macchia"* (A spot), are thrown off as if she were puzzled to be discovering the blood on her hand, as if saying, "Where did this come from?"

To create again what Verdi was telling his singers in those long rehearsals, Marilyn Feller Somville reads Verdi's expressive markings in the score through the advice Verdi was giving in his letters. For instance:

The indication *soffocata e lento* in Macbeth's *Tutto è finito* [All is over], just before the duet *Fatal mia donna,* requires, in addition to covering the voice, the sobbing effect (accompanied by quick *coups de glotte*)—strong gestures conveying to us Macbeth's recoil from so much bloodshed and his ineptness as a murderer. (M 242–43)

This may seem a lot to read into a few syllables, but that is the kind of vivid drama Verdi was aiming for, and it alone explains the hours of rehearsal he spent trying to make his singers "not sing," but live entirely in the dramatic situation. Giorgio Strehler, the great director, even claimed that Verdi's detailed instructions to his singers "anticipate the devices of modern theater by a whole century."[8]

Another example from Somville:

The indication *con trasporto* for Lady's *O voluttà del soglio! O scettro* [O voluptuous throne! O scepter] (the final section of her aria in Act II of the revised opera) required some of those "yells" (maximum chest quality, *voce piena*) which quickly calm down to *pp* and a wavering tone (*oscillante*)—crucial gestures by which Verdi delineates in the revision a more subtle Lady, one whose excessive and glutted ambition renders her vulnerable to self-doubt long before the sleepwalking scene. (M 243)

The reason Verdi did not want "fine singers" is that he doubted he could prod such almost feral sounds from them, as he could from Varesi and Barbieri.

Notes

1. Charlotte Carmichael Stopes, *Burbage and Shakespeare's Stage* (University Press of the Pacific, 1913), p. 108.
2. Quoted in T. W. Baldwin, *The Organization and Personnel of the Shakespearean Company* (Russell & Russell, 1961), p. 423.
3. In a fourth play, *King Lear* (3.4), Edgar pretends to be bewitched by devils named Flibbertigibbet, Smulkin, and Modo.
4. Tadolini, a regular performer of Rossini, Donizetti, and Bellini, sang in Verdi's *I Lombardi, Ernani, Alzira,* and *Attila.*
5. Gaetano Ferri had sung successfully in Verdi's *Nabucco* (1842) and would create the role of Edgardo in his *Aroldo* (1857).
6. Though Verdi kept the English form, *Macbeth,* for the title of his opera, in the body of the work he uses the Italian forms Macbetto and Banco.
7. Writing of Shirley Verrett's performance as Lady Macbeth in Giorgio Strehler's production of the opera, a *Time* magazine reviewer criticized Verrett's "bland unchanging facial expression" in the sleepwalking scene. Clearly, Verrett had read Verdi's instructions for the scene. The *Time* reviewer had not.
8. Giorgio Strehler, *Corriere d'Informazione,* November 1, 1973.

2

Diabolisms, Old and New

Shakespeare's *Macbeth* (1606) was perhaps the thirtieth of the thirty-eight plays written solely or mainly by him, and he was forty-two years old when his company presented it. The play comes between such towering creations as *King Lear* and *Antony and Cleopatra*.

Verdi's *Macbeth* (1847) was the tenth of his twenty-seven operas, written when he was thirty-three. The opera stands out in the company of his early works, but he had not yet reached his glorious period (that of *Rigoletto, La Traviata, Il Trovatore*)—so he would rewrite it in 1864 to incorporate the strengths he had acquired by then. But even in its first form it was a great success and a breakthrough in Verdi's quest for tight musical drama.

The resemblances between *Macbeth* the play and *Macbeth* the opera are clear, but not all of them are obvious. They both deal with witchcraft and the devil. They both have a politics of usurpation and nationalistic yearnings. Less obvious is the fact that they are both quite short entries in the canon of their respective creators, and both draw on comparatively restricted resources. *Macbeth*, without Middleton's Hecate songs added to it, is the second-shortest play we have from Shakespeare. Only *The Comedy of Errors* is shorter. The rest of the shorter plays by Shakespeare are comedies, leaving time for music and slapstick. *Macbeth* is the only tragedy in that company.

It is a two-boy play, and one boy has only a scatter of small appearances—Fleance for two lines, young Macduff for twenty-one lines, the "gentlewoman" in the sleepwalking scene for another twenty-one, and one apparition for five lines (John Rice would have to take the eight-line appearance of the other apparition). This quadrupling of roles shows what was meant by the earlier reference to an actor septupling roles, a thing that could happen only when the roles were snippets.

The logic of doubling keeps Lady Macbeth off the stage for the interval in which John Rice plays Lady Macduff. In modern productions, women play the witches, but boys did not take those parts for Shakespeare—he did not have three boys at the time. The unnatural quality of the witches is underlined by the fact that adult males play them, as we learn from Banquo:

> What are these
> So wither'd and so wild in their attire,
> That look not like th' inhabitants o' th' earth,
> And yet are on't? Live you? or are you aught
> That man may question? You seem to understand me,
> By each at once her choppy finger laying
> Upon her skinny lips. You should be women,
> And yet your beards forbid me to interpret
> That you are so. (1.3.39–47)

The manly witches perfectly express the inversion of nature that witches represent.

Verdi's *Macbeth*, similarly, is a short opera, especially before the additions made for the Paris production. There is only a small part for the tenor Macduff. The king who is killed is not given a singing part at all, nor is Fleance. Macduff's wife and child are entirely eliminated, as is the Porter. Verdi himself described his narrow focus in the work: "Above all, bear in mind that there are three roles in this opera, and three is all there can be.—Lady Macbeth, Macbeth, and the chorus of witches" (M 99).

The importance of the witches is obvious. Both play and opera begin with them. The protagonist in each engages in criminal necromancy with them, trying to learn the future from "The instruments of darkness" (1.3.124), a thing forbidden by civil and ecclesiastical law in both cultures. It is clear that the diabolism of play and opera appealed to the audiences of their separate times, as we can tell by other works written and performed around them. But the atmosphere of the two diabolisms is quite different, more theological and political in Shakespeare's Renaissance, more gothic and Romantic in Verdi's period.

Shakespeare: Renaissance Diabolism

Shakespeare could count on his audience's absolute belief in witches. His government was still hanging them, and King James had personally interrogated witches, passed laws against them, and written a treatise on them (*Daemonologie*). As Dr. Johnson wrote, Shakespeare "was far from overburdening the credulity of his audience. . . . The goblins of witchcraft still continued to hover in the twilight."[1] The hard edge of combat with the devil in King James's England is manifest in Barnabe Barnes's play *The Devil's Charter,* put on by Shakespeare's troupe before King James at the beginning of 1607. The play is about the corrupt court of Pope Alexander VI and his bastard children. The pope comes into one scene carrying a "lintstock" for firing explosives. No audience could see this early in 1607 and not have in mind the linstock Guy Fawkes and his fellow Catholics had brought into the vault of Parliament for blowing up the king and all his government late in 1605. That close call meant that anti-Catholicism was not just an idle prejudice in the court season of 1606–7. It was a panicky reaction on the part of people fighting for their lives. The Gunpowder Plot did not succeed, but it did set off an explosion of sorts, a storm of polemical sermons, pamphlets, poems, and plays denouncing the plotters, their sponsors, their religion, their treachery, and their pope.

The Master of the Revels normally ruled out contemporary political references, but a national crisis—especially one prompted by Catholic challenge—could lead to a loosening of the rules. That had happened when the Spanish Armada threatened England in 1588. A series of "Armada plays" was allowed by the Master. In 1606—the year following the exposure of the Gunpowder Plot—there was a wave of Powder plays, anti-Catholic tales of diabolical scheming, using many key words from the anti-Powder sermons and pamphlets, words like "train" (as verb for the gunpowder fuse) and "vault" (where the gunpowder was lodged). At least four plays fit this pattern—John Marston's *Sophonisba*, Thomas Dekker's *The Whore of Babylon*, Barnabe Barnes's *The Devil's Charter*, and *Macbeth*. They all involve forms of witchcraft prompted by the devil—which is how the government saw the Plot. The Jesuits who knew of the Plot were accused of celebrating the oath to kill the king at a Black Mass.

Macbeth is not normally considered a Powder play, since it is subtler than the other propagandistic dramas. But it is in some ways the timeliest of them all. It was celebrated before the Scottish king who was the object of the intended murder (just as Duncan is in the play). It was produced not only a year following

the Plot's discovery but seven months after the trial of the man
considered the evil genius of the Plot, Jesuit superior Henry Garnet, and just months before a government campaign to find a
"relic" from Father Garnet's "martyrdom."

The trial of Garnet focused largely on his treatise defending
equivocation, the use of true statements meant to deceive. The
witches are treated throughout *Macbeth* as equivocators. Indeed,
Banquo indicts them with what could be a textbook definition of
equivocation by diabolical forces:

> And oftentimes, to win us to our harm,
> The instruments of darkness tell us truths,
> Win us with honest trifles, to betray's
> In deepest consequence. (1.3.123–26)

Too late, Macbeth will experience the force of this definition.
He at last comes to recognize "th' equivocation of the fiend/
That lies like truth" (5.5.42–43). He denounces his own earlier
belief in the witches:

> And be these juggling fiends no more believ'd
> That palter with us in a double sense,
> That keep the word of promise to our ear,
> And break it to our hope. (5.8.19–22)

The theme of equivocation is everywhere in the play, in a
day when "foul is fair" (1.1.11), in the battle that is "lost and won"
(1.1.4), in the witches who are neither female nor male (1.3.45–46),
in their news that "Cannot be ill; cannot be good" (1.3.131), in a
devil who can "speak true" (1.3.107), in "instruments of darkness

tell us truths" (1.3.124), in Lady Macbeth who is a woman yet "unsex[ed]" (1.5.41), in a castle blessed with "heaven's breath" (1.6.5) that is a gate to hell (2.3.2), in a dagger that is there and not there (2.1.35), in a dawn that is not a dawn (2.4.6–9 and 3.4.125–26), in Malcolm's "welcome and unwelcome" words (4.3.138), in a Birnam forest that walks (4.1.93–94), in Macduff's birth that was not a birth (5.8.15–16), even in the effects of drink:

> Lechery, sir, it provokes, and unprovokes: it provokes the desire, but it takes away the performance. Therefore much drink may be said to be an *equivocator* with lechery: it makes him, and it mars him; it sets him on, and it takes him off; it persuades him, and disheartens him; makes him stand to, and not stand to; in conclusion, *equivocates* him in a sleep, and giving him the lie, leaves him. (2.3.29–36)

But the centerpiece of all these references to equivocation is a slashing attack on Henry Garnet himself. It comes in a pyrotechnical display of references in the Porter's speech (2.3.1–21) that make sense only in connection with the trial of Garnet and the multiple attacks on him in 1606. These digs are delivered by the comic specialist of the time, Robert Armin, not only an actor but a playwright, a pamphleteer, and a theorist of jesting.[2] There has been endless and fruitless controversy over the references in the Porter's speech as the self-proclaimed gatekeeper of hell (an inverse Saint Peter at the gates of heaven). He seems to welcome three sinners into the everlasting bonfire. Actually, he proclaims three titles for the entrant—as the witches gave Macbeth three titles (Glamis, Cawdor, King) though he was only one person (another form of equivocation).

The first title is "farmer" (2.3.4). Father Garnet's assumed name in his disguise was Farmer—which he took as an equivocal "truth," since he came to harvest souls. As the Porter says, he acted "on th' expectation of plenty." He adds that he will "Have napkins enow about you, here you'll sweat for' it." The Porter is mocking the Catholics who pushed up to the platform where Garnet's body was disassembled in the heavy butchery of being hanged, drawn, and quartered, and dipped their napkins in his blood to take home as relics. The total exsanguination of several bodies at a time made the gallows a river of blood. When Macbeth looks at the blood on his hands and calls them "these hangman's hands" (2.2.25), it can puzzle a modern audience that thinks of the hangman as simply handling a noose. Macbeth is thinking of the hangman who quarters bodies with an ax, splashing blood all over himself.

The second title given by the Porter is "equivocator, that could swear in both the scales against either scale, who committed treason enough for God's sake, yet could not equivocate to heaven" (2.3.8–11). There is a consensus that this refers to Garnet.

The third title bestowed by the Porter has confounded almost all editors. The title is "tailor" (2.3.13), and most critics think he is in hell for skimping fabric in his trade—a strange sin to be ranked with the others. Only H. L. Rogers discovered the point of this third title.[3] The Catholics had boasted of a great miracle coming out of Garnet's execution. While others at the execution of Garnet took away blood on their handkerchiefs, one man took away a bit of straw on which Garnet's blood had fallen, forming (it was claimed) the image of his own face. This miraculous straw became famous, and just months after *Macbeth* was first performed the government launched a massive search for it, to discredit the miracle. Royal agents raided a tailor's shop where it had been—an exploit celebrated in a polemical poem, "The Jesuits' Miracles," where the tailor was called a "skipping silkman." In official accounts of the raid, the tailor is called a "goseman," after the "goose" (iron) he used on his garments. The Porter says (of hell), "here you may roast your goose" (2.3.14–15). Garnet is greeted with the title of the man who kept his relic, the "skipping silkman." The welcoming of Garnet into hell is an inversion of the witches' welcoming of Macbeth into their magic circle. They conjure up images from below. The Porter creates a conjuration down into the underworld.

The Porter scene was attacked by Coleridge as "disgusting," something Shakespeare could not have written.[4] He said it had to come from "some other hand," not Shakespeare's. Those who did not similarly condemn it as low and trivial tried to excuse it as "comic relief"—though there is a deadly truth in the fact that Macbeth and his wife have turned their castle into a hell, where hell's gatekeeper welcomes sinners. Thomas De Quincey, in his famous essay "On the Knocking at the Gate in *Macbeth*," defended the scene as a reflux of the ordinary world after the dark sequence of the murder—an odd view of the imagined hell of the Porter's words.[5] In point of fact, both his greeting of Garnet and his speech on drink as an equivocator tie the Porter tightly into the polemical purpose of the work. It is savage in its humor. There is a current tendency to find Shakespeare a crypto-Catholic. I cannot think that this savage treatment of Garnet, so soon after his cruel butchering, could come from even a semi-Catholic. It goes beyond anything Shakespeare might have been tempted to in stoking James's hatred of Jesuits (the

king conducted a long doctrinal polemic with the famous Italian
Jesuit Roberto Bellarmino).

The Porter scene is a rather small role for Robert Armin, the
troupe's clown of the time. That is why many think Armin doubled the third witch, the one who shares a "familiar" with Lady
Macbeth. Armin as one of the witches gives a special weight to
his role as Porter, a keeper of the infernal regions, welcoming
down the equivocating Garnet as the witches welcome up the
tempted Macbeth. The play is a savage indictment of Renaissance diabolism, never more so than in the Porter scene.

The play moves through darkness and "the dunnest smoke of
hell" (1.5.51). It is a night piece, played under a starless sky: "Hell
is murky" (5.1.36). Only Macbeth and Banquo meet the witches.
Lady Macbeth never does. But she does not need to. She is a witch
herself. She has called on the patron devils of murder to invert
nature in her, to "unsex" her, to empty out all human feelings,
stop up the passage to remorse, block the very circulation of her
blood, drain her of milk and replace it with gall (the liquid with
which witches nursed their familiars), stuff her emptied body full
from top to toe with "direst cruelty" (1.5.40–54).

This ecstatic reveling in evil, this orgy of hate, is such that
modern actresses often deliver it squirming on a couch or bed
as they reach orgasm. This may seem sensationalistic, but in
Shakespeare's day it was regularly thought that witches had
intercourse with the devil, or with their familiars. It is appropriate that, in making herself incapable of sex in the normal human
way, she should be mated unnaturally with her new patron.
Other actresses show the erotics of hell in different ways. At the
Chicago Shakespeare Theater, Karen Aldridge delivered this

speech topless. Judi Dench, in Trevor Nunn's version, invoked the devils by holding a supplicating hand just above the earth as she gave the lines. Sarah Siddons, the great eighteenth-century interpreter of the role, said she was undergoing diabolical possession in this speech.[6]

Lady Macbeth is relying, she tells us, on "metaphysical aid" (1.5.29) to accomplish her goals, and her husband's. "Metaphysical" here means "supernatural," in the diabolic sense—what Verdi meant by "fantastic" power. In the sleepwalking scene (5.1), the Folio direction is: "Enter Lady, with a Taper." Walking with a taper was the regular punishment of a witch, as Shakespeare told us in 2 Henry VI, where the Duchess of Gloucester is penalized for witchcraft. The Folio stage direction there is "Enter the Duchesse barefoot, in a white Sheet, and a Taper burning in her hand" (2.4). The stage direction for Lady Macbeth does not mention the white sheet, but the "Waiting-Gentlewoman" has told us she does "throw her night-gown upon her" (5.1.5), and the sleepwalking scene is always performed barefoot—so the picture is exactly the same for the Duchess-witch and the Lady-witch.[7] She is already in hell as she speaks, recognizing that "Hell is murky" (5.1.36).

⸱ Gothic Diabolism

Nineteenth-century opera was a Romantic Era product—tending toward a Byronic *nostalgie de la boue*, with madness, curses, ruins, hermits, cloisters, magic potions, suicide, and ghosts often at hand. It had in its DNA the gothic novels of the eighteenth century and such nineteenth-century practitioners as Edgar Allan Poe and the Brontë sisters. It could, like the Renaissance diabolism of

Shakespeare, have an anti-Catholic strain, as in Poe's tale "The Pit and the Pendulum" or Verdi's opera *Don Carlos*, but this was not a matter of theological rigor, as in the anti-Garnet propaganda of the Powder plays. It was indulging a shudder toward the exotic, an aesthetic of scariness. We are moving, here, the distance from Marlowe's *Dr. Faustus* (1592?) to Louis Spohr's *Faust* (1816).

Nineteenth-century opera, as a product of the Romantic Era, is thus gothic in a general sense, full of melancholy, terror, and cemeteries; but *Macbeth* figures in a more specific subset of the gothic, that of the devil story. By the time of *Macbeth* (1847), there were two touchstones of the *fantastico*—Carl Maria von Weber's *Der Freischütz* (1821) and Giacomo Meyerbeer's *Robert le Diable* (1831)—with which *Macbeth* was instantly compared. Verdi knew this would be the case. The Teatro della Pergola that premiered his opera in Florence had just run revivals of *Freischütz* and *Robert*. When the revised *Macbeth* was premiered at the Théâtre-Lyrique in Paris, it was pitted against the old favorite *Robert le Diable,* being performed at the same time in the Paris Opéra (L 1.xii, xvi, xxvi).

Verdi realized he was encroaching on such turf from the outset. As he told the theater manager of the Pergola: "The subject is neither political nor religious, it is fantastical" (M 5). That is the term used for gothic forms, and it was the term used against him in early reviews of the Florence premiere. The leading Florentine music critics—Abramo Basevi, Enrico Montazio, Luigi Ferdinando Casamorata—had some good things to say about the opera, but they agreed that Verdi failed *in genere fantastico* (M 141–42, 232–33). Only the northerners, it was said, had the true Romantic shiver. Basevi, the best of the critics, wrote a series of articles on the opera and then published them in his book on

Verdi. He tried to warn Verdi away from any more exercises in the demonic:

> Following the example of various celebrated transalpine masters, Verdi determined to set a fantastic or pagan supernatural subject. Neither the success of Meyerbeer or Weber in this genre of music, nor a certain aversion of Italian composers to setting this sort of extraordinary plot, served to make Verdi avoid the dangerous risk. I say dangerous because the fantastic genre, of transalpine birth and character, requires music appropriate to its nature, and so the Italian composer must abandon the beaten paths which he knows so well to venture into a labyrinth in which the northern genius may wander without losing his way. (M 421)

The witches were the thing that troubled these critics most. They were called trivial or comic, without the spooky authenticity of Weber's diabolical agent (Caspar) or Meyerbeer's (Bertram). Such characters were considered more dignified than the witches—the devil is a gentleman, and there is nothing gentlewomanly about the witches. As parallels to Caspar and Bertram in Verdi, it is true, the witches will not do. For that, one must go in Verdi to demonic figures like Sparafucile, the Grand Inquisitor, or Jago. On the other hand, we do have a dignified witch in *Macbeth*—Lady Macbeth.

The Florentine critics wanted Byronic gloom, not Shakespearean grotesques. For the witches in Shakespeare *are* grotesque. The distinctive thing about witches is the way they combine communication with their dread lords, the enemies of all mankind, and their mean little maliciousnesses, like turning a cow's milk sour or quarreling with a peasant woman over chestnuts

(*Macbeth* 1.3.4–6). Verdi was right to include both these aspects of Shakespeare's witches. His general treatment is to issue dread chords of doom in the orchestra, followed by cackling scampers of the witches, with crippled emphases on the offbeat. The interplay of the menacing and the trivial is itself a form of equivocation—what seem to be two meanings are made one in the disfigured slyness of the witches, more dangerous than they seem. Julian Budden deftly describes the witches' first chorus:

> The sense of weirdness is conveyed by the unrelieved minor tonality, hollow harmonies, shrill orchestration, grace-notes, irregularity of bar structure, and at one point, at the words *Ma lo sposo,* a displacement of the main accent from the first to the third beat of the line. If all this does not add up to anything very terrifying, it at least recognizes the essentially childish malice of the witches in the [Shakespeare] play. (B 2.82)

Verdi at first wanted the witch chorus to be made up entirely of sopranos, no contraltos, so they could have a more cackling sonority, abetted at times by sinister low woodwinds, at other times by shrieking high ones. The weird effects he sought in the witches' music reach a climax in the eerie processional he composed for the line of Banco's heirs revealed to Macbetto in the Weird Sisters' lair. For this he had a *banda* play beneath the stage, under the trapdoor from which Banco's ghost rises (M 67). Budden says of this effect:

> From the combination of two oboes, six clarinets, two bassoons and one contrabassoon, placed under the stage, he contrived one of the most unearthly sounds in nineteenth

century opera, all the more disconcerting for the simplicity
of the music itself. (B 1.303)

It is coming to seem a historical curiosity that the Florentine
critics preferred Weber's Wolf's Glen and Meyerbeer's ruined
convent to Verdi's cauldron. (Meyerbeer summoned from the
convent the ghosts of lecherous nuns who dance a bacchanal and
a ballet of seduction.) As early as 1894, Bernard Shaw tells us, London audiences tittered through the Halloween "oogie-boogie" of
the Wolf's Glen.[8] Though Verdi's *Macbeth* went through a period
of comparative neglect, it has in modern times been performed
more often, and to more appreciative critics, than have those
other works. There is nothing in them to equal the psychological depths musically plumbed in Macbetto and his wife, and the
working of their two psyches is put in motion, after all, by the
witches.

Verdi said that the impact of the witches should be felt all
through the opera, not just in the scenes where they appear
(M 99). He gave them an extra appearance, after the *duettino* between Macbetto and Banco in Act 1, which has the effect of wrap-
ping them around Macbetto's first reaction to their prophecies.
Many modern productions try to show the witches' continuing
influence by having them silently appear at various points, especially at the end of the play or opera, as overseers of the doom
they predicted. Shakespeare, of course, could not do this, since
the adults who played the witches were needed for other roles,
especially around the battle scenes at the end. Trevor Nunn, in his
1976 production, had all the actors all the time sit around a great
circle, inside which the scenes were played out. So the witches are
always there, even when they are not in the circle.

There is no denying that modern audiences, not assisted by theology or folklore as Shakespeare and Verdi were, have trouble knowing what to make of the witches. The problem is to make them exotic and unnatural, yet to find a plausible reason for them to come near more civilized people. Shakespeare explained their presence at the uncivilized site of a battle, where they can cull hacked body parts for use in their cauldron. They cannot steal from corpses in consecrated cemeteries—that is why they must scavenge the unblessed bodies of men fallen in their sins. They must steer clear of all the weapons used against them—crucifixes and signs of the cross, holy water, religious medals, rosary beads, and other church paraphernalia.[9] Witches can raid bodies not blessed by the church—unbaptized babies (4.1.30–31), or Jews (4.1.26), or Turks and Tartars (4.1.29). Rifling the gallows (4.1.66) or shipwrecks (1.3.29) is another "safe" activity. But this doctrinal view of witches is hardly part of the modern audience's mental stock.

Modern directors, whether of the play or of the opera, clearly feel uncomfortable with the witches, and rack their brains for ways to make them convincing. In Giorgio Strehler's 1975 production of the opera, which I saw during its Washington, D.C., run, the stage was covered with a thick fabric, heaving as by earthquake, and the witches emerged from it like chthonic spirits. The BBC television *Macbeth* did something similar. The curled-up witches seemed, at their first appearance, to be rocks on the landscape—until they straightened up into their human form. That is one of two modern trends. The first treats them as prehistoric or primitive. Strehler connected his subterranean witches with Freud's subconscious.[10] Other directors, too, have tried to make them expressions of Freud's id (with the urges of ambition rather than sex). They are fairly often shown as naked "cave women" (scampering on all fours, like gorillas, in the Claude d'Anna production under Riccardo Chailly's baton). Orson Welles made them voodoo priestesses (on stage) or Druids (on screen). The Barcelona opera house presented them as sibyls. Trevor Nunn had a drooling idiot girl receive the prophecies— the other two witches were her keepers. The mad theme was taken to its extreme in Zurich, where Thomas Hampson sang Macbeth and the witches were insane inmates of an asylum— what on earth took Macbeth there to meet them?

A second trend, far from the primitive school, makes the witches parasites on the modern scene. They have been shown as groupies, who flock to Macbeth as to a rock star. Sam Worthington's modernized version of the play made the witches a drug gang's molls. In the 2008 Broadway production by director Rupert Goold, with Patrick Stewart playing Macbeth, the witches were field nurses who killed rather than healed their patients. The Chicago Shakespeare Theater made them *paparazze*. In 2007 the Metropolitan Opera presented them as bag ladies. Others have shown them as begging gypsies. This makes them the kind of nuisances one meets in an airport (like LaRouchies or Hare Krishnas). One problem with this approach is that it makes the witches pursue Macbeth, but in the play and the opera they wait for him to come to them.

The witches do not pester Macbeth, or tell him what to do. At their first meeting they hail him solemnly, each hail rising higher to salute one of his new titles in the opera. After that initial greeting, he pesters them, while they put up at least token resistance. He seeks them out in their lair. We are not told how he knew where that lair was. One can suppose he followed a magnetic attraction in his psyche.

In the case of the opera (as opposed to the play) the sense of cluster or pursuit may have been prompted by the fact that Verdi turned the three witches into a whole chorus of them. Yet he insisted the witches should form three different units of six, even when singing in combination (M 33). His directions for the entry chorus read: "Enter the threefold troupe of witches. All the witches are present, but each group must be kept distinct from the other" (L 1.18–20). Eighteen was his original number for the chorus—additional singers make it more difficult to keep the three groups separate. The chorus is not one "coven," but three, since there is order in hell. This note of discipline disappears if what we see is a mad scramble of *paparazze* or bag ladies. Barbara Gaines, in her 2010 production for the Chicago Lyric Opera, emphasized the tripartite nature of the chorus by having the three main witches fly in to join the other singers, in successive "flights" on wire.

The witches are too jolly for some tastes, as in their giddily swirling dance just before Macbeth first enters, "Le sorrele vagabonde": "The roaming sisters flit across the waves, skilled to weave a circle enclosing land and sea." They seem to be having too much fun. But Dante, as opposed to Milton, showed that there can be humor (if of a self-lacerating kind) in hell. The Mephistopheles of the various Faust operas laughs defiantly and sings humorous songs. It is true that he does not giggle, as some of the witches' music suggests. But witches are lower in hell's social order than Mephistopheles. Modern directors must keep searching for a modern diabolism, at a time when that category is less defined than it was in the Renaissance or the Romantic Era.

Notes

1. *Johnson on Shakespeare,* edited by Arthur Sherbo (Yale University Press, 1968), pp. 3, 5.
2. Armin's various writings were gathered in two volumes by J. P. Feather as *The Collected Works of Robert Armin* (Johnson Reprint Company, 1972).
3. H. L. Rogers, "An English Tailor and Father Garnet's Straw," *Review of English Studies* (1965), pp. 44–49.
4. *Coleridge's Criticism of Shakespeare: A Selection,* edited by R. A. Foakes (Athlone Press, 1989), p. 103.
5. Thomas De Quincey, *Confessions of an English Opium-Eater and Other Writings,* edited by Grevel Lindop (Oxford University Press, 1996), pp. 81–86.
6. Sarah Siddons, "Remarks on the Character of Lady Macbeth," in Thomas Campbell, *The Life of Mrs. Siddons* (E. Wilson, 1834), vol. 2, pp. 11–12. The Lady Macbeth of Mrs. Siddons was admired by leading writers of her time—Richard Brinsley Sheridan, William Hazlitt, Leigh Hunt, Samuel Johnson, and others.
7. Roman Polanski, in his 1971 film *Macbeth,* had his Lady Macbeth sleepwalk in the nude. At the premiere of the movie, I asked Polanski if he did not think the witch references to gown and taper were important. He referred me to his artistic adviser standing by, the critic Kenneth Tynan, who blithely assured me that Shakespeare would have done the scene nude except for the fact that *his* Lady Macbeth was a boy. I remarked that I had been in Scottish castles, whose interiors are cold and wet even in summer, and they hardly invite anyone to nudity.
8. *Shaw on Music,* edited by Eric Bentley (Applause Books, 1983), pp. 94–95.
9. For religious objects as warders-off of witches, see Keith Thomas, the great expert on the occult, *Religion and the Decline of Magic* (Penguin, 1979), pp. 561–62, 589–90. He argues that belief in such holy objects made Catholic lands less susceptible to witch scares than Protestant countries, which forbade the objects.
10. David L. Hirst, *Giorgio Strehler* (Cambridge University Press, 1993), p. 75.

3
Psychological Depth

Verdi was clearly drawn to *Macbeth* because of the psychological depth found in its leading characters.

≀ *Shakespeare*

The Macbeths, husband and wife, are divided within themselves, and those inner divisions divide them from each other. Macbeth backs himself toward the murder, protesting that he will not do it, cannot do it, but moving inexorably in that direction. From the minute when the third witch predicts that he will be king, he knows that he will murder Duncan. He does not trust the witches because one prediction has come true, that he is now Thane of Cawdor. He trusts them because he knows he will murder the king. He is like Raskolnikov in *Crime and Punishment*, who just knows, from page 1 of the novel, that he will kill the pawn-dealer woman.

The witches do not tell Macbeth how he will become king, just that he will. There are many possible ways for him to reach the throne—illness or the accidental death of Duncan or Malcolm, political maneuvering, revolution, a palace coup. Macbeth gives a cursory nod in that direction:

> If chance will have me king, why, chance may crown me
> Without my stir. (1.3.143–44)

But that is just a notional aside, which causes no real reaction in him, as opposed to the thought that instantly seizes, rattles, and oppresses him—the certitude that he will advance by murder:

> why do I yield to that suggestion
> Whose horrid image doth unfix my hair
> And make my seated heart knock at my ribs,
> Against the use of nature? Present fears
> Are less than horrible imaginings:
> My thought, whose murther yet is but fantastical [imagined],
> Shakes so my single state of man that function
> Is smother'd in surmise, and nothing is
> But what is not. (1.3.134–42)

On the one hand, Macbeth ticks off the reasons why he should not kill the king:

> He's here in double trust:
> First, as I am his kinsman and his subject,
> Strong both against the deed; then, as his host,
> Who should against his murtherer shut the door,
> Not bear the knife myself. (1.7.12–16)

But that is what his full consciousness is saying. His subconscious is far stronger, as he shudders toward his goal. This is perfectly expressed in the dagger that he imagines leading him: "Thou marshal'st me the way that I was going" (2.1.42). He follows this "dagger of the mind" as if hypnotized by his own imagination.

Macbeth's wife has a first reaction to the idea of murder very different from that of her husband. As we have seen, she exults orgasmically at the prospect. This is the beginning of a counter-pointed relationship that traces asymmetric arcs—she professing fearlessness while doubts eat at her, he professing horror as he moves to his task. They will gradually change places, he becoming impervious to feelings while she falls apart.

The early critics of Verdi's opera deplored the lack of a love story in it. The husband and wife are bound together not in love, but in ambition. In modern therapy-speak, they are each other's "enablers." When Macbeth expresses admiration for her—"Bring forth men-children only!" (1.7.72)—it is for the prospect of giving him male heirs of her mettle. She is afraid at the outset that he has too much of the milk of human kindness in him to accomplish their purpose. After he says, "We will proceed no further," she lashes him on:

> Was the hope drunk
> Wherein you dress'd yourself? Hath it slept since?
> And wakes it now to look so green and pale
> At what it did so freely? From this time
> Such I account thy love. (1.7.35–39)

There could be no clearer statement that her "love" waits entirely on Macbeth's ability to satisfy her ambition. It is significant that, both in the play and in the opera, Macbeth laments the loss of all love before he learns of his wife's death:

> And that which should accompany old age,
> As honor, *love,* obedience, troops of friends,
> I must not look to have. (5.3.24–26)[1]

He still seems to falter when he says, "If we should fail?" The best actress I have ever heard as Lady Macbeth, Judith Anderson,

replied: *"WE? FAIL? But-screw-your-courage-to-the-sticking-place,
and WE'LL / NOT / FAIL"* (1.7.59–61). All the macho that should
be the male's seems to belong to her at this point. She even
takes Duncan's blood and "gilds" the faces of the grooms with it
when Macbeth is too terrified to return to the scene of his crime
(2.2.52–53).

She keeps her role as murder's cheerleader when Macbeth
expresses horror at his hangman's hands:

> My hands are of your color; but I shame
> To wear a heart so white. (2.2.61–62)

Later, at the banquet, when Macbeth shouts at Banquo's
ghost, she whispers fiercely, "Are you a man?" (3.4.57). She calls
him "Shame itself!" and says he is like a weak old woman (while
she is like a bold young man):

> O, these flaws and starts
> (Impostors to true fear) would well become
> A woman's story at a winter's fire,
> Authoriz'd by her grandam. Shame itself,
> Why do you make such faces? (3.4.62–66)

But there are signs that under her bravado the woman is protesting too much. After getting the grooms drunk, she boasts,
"That which hath made them drunk hath made me bold"
(2.2.1)—only to almost jump out of her skin at the hooting of an
owl (2.2.2–3). She leaves the killing to Macbeth, having faltered
herself, knife in hand, as she looked at the sleeping Duncan:

> Had he not resembled
> My father as he slept, I had done't. (2.2.12–13)

She reveals in her sleepwalking what she was thinking as she gilded the grooms' faces with Duncan's blood: "Yet who would have thought the old man to have had SO MUCH BLOOD in him?" (5.1.39–40). There is an inadvertent admission that she shares Macbeth's fears when she says;

These deeds must not be thought
After these ways; so, it will make *us* mad. (2.2.30–31)

When the court gathers after the murder and expresses its horror, she faints and must be carried out (2.3.125). It used to be said that Lady Macbeth was pretending to faint, to distract people from Macbeth's weak defense of his killing the grooms. But acting this is difficult—how does she fool the characters on the stage, but not the audience out front? Those who took this interpretation almost always had to add something to the scene to make it clear, and if that had been what Shakespeare wanted, he would have added it himself. Rather, the disintegration of Lady Macbeth, already hinted at in the text, is proceeding toward its culmination in her suicide.[2] Judith Anderson said she reacted to Macbeth's claim that he had killed the grooms, whom she had just "gilded" with blood: "She faints because she can't help it. . . . She hears him say he has killed the two grooms, something that was not in their plan. Already the deed has got beyond her."[3] If Lady Macbeth were calculating and in control, she would not want to be carried out, where she could not track the course of events and make her own intervention.

Macbeth begins to move out from Lady Macbeth's control when he refuses to tell her he has arranged for Banquo's murder: "Be innocent of the knowledge, dearest chuck" (3.2.45). After the banquet, as he determines "to know, / By the worst means, the worst" (3.4.133–34), he no longer consults with his wife, just with the witches. He does not let her in on his murdering of Lady Macduff and her children. He goes from the man who trembled at the very thought of murder to a person who is insensible to fear or any other feelings. Lady Macbeth had pled with devils to empty her of her femininity. He has succeeded in draining himself of feelings, and of humanity:

> The time has been, my senses would have cool'd
> To hear a night-shriek, and my fell of hair
> Would at a dismal treatise rouse and stir
> As life were in't. I have supp'd full with horrors;
> Direness, familiar to my slaughterous thoughts,
> Cannot once start me. (5.5.10–15)

Auden says that Macbeth, in trying to see future time through the witches' words, has erased time, made it a blur of indistinguishable things lacking nature's logic:

> The consequence of the wish to control the future, for both Macbeth and Lady Macbeth, is to destroy the significance of time completely. . . . The whole sequence of past, present, and future is broken for them, and so, too, is the circular revolution of natural time, of sleeping and waking.[4]

Told of his wife's death, Macbeth remains affectless. There is no framework in which to place this event, or any other:

> There would have been a time for such a word.
> To-morrow, and to-morrow, and to-morrow,
> Creeps in this petty pace from day to day,

To the last syllable of recorded time;
And all our yesterdays have lighted fools
The way to dusty death. Out, out, brief candle!
Life's but a walking shadow, a poor player,
That struts and frets his hour upon the stage,
And then is heard no more. It is a tale
Told by an idiot, full of sound and fury,
Signifying nothing. (5.5.18–28)

The two become walking shells, hollowed out. In order to kill others, they have had to kill themselves and each other, in their depths. Lady Macbeth expresses more truth than she knows when she says:

'Tis safer to be that which we destroy
Than by destruction dwell in doubtful joy. (3.2.6–7)

⟨ *Verdi*

Verdi understood very well the divided psyches Shakespeare provided him with. Macbetto and his wife talk past each other, not to each other, hiding from each other, and each hiding from him- or herself. It is all there in the music. It is there in the *duettino* that Verdi asked Varesi to accept in place of an entrance aria, the comments of Macbetto and Banco after they have encountered the witches in Act I.

Duettino

This is not a real duet between Macbetto and Banco but overlapping soliloquies. Macbetto is musing on power, and Banco is musing on Macbetto's musings. Macbetto begins,

Due vaticini compiuti or sono
Mi si promette dal terzo un trono.
[Two predictions already fulfilled,
By the third is promised me a throne.]

Verdi told Varesi these lines should be delivered in quizzical bewilderment (*"fra sè, sotto voce quasi con ispavento,"* to himself, in lowered voice, as if in fright). But then he starts to bluster (*con esclamazione*):

MA PERCHÉ SENTO . . .
[Then why do I feel . . .]

The first three syllables (*"Ma perché"*) have vertical accent marks, as if they should be "punched." The *"sento"* has a diminuendo marking, preparatory to shivering off in the next line, with a soft hollow voice (*à voce cupa*):

. . . rizzarsi il crine
[. . . stands up my hair?]

Here the syllables are divided into two notes, the second one dropping a tone, as if he were shrinking away from the symptoms he is feeling ("sta-ands u-up my-ee hair"). The first line (*"Ma perché sento"*) bravely begins a question which the second is afraid to answer. Then he repeats the bold rise and the timid descent, but this time a tone lower, as if his boldness is slipping:

PENSIER DI SANGUE
d'onde sei nato?

[PROSPECT OF BLOOD
whe-ence do-oo you-oo come from?]

Verdi was insistent that Varesi get this dynamic in all its sub-
tleties, since it already shows us a man deeply divided, almost
sundered in two:

> Bear well in mind the dramatic situation, which is when he
> meets the witches who predict the throne for him. You are
> stunned and terrified by the prophecy; but, at the same time,
> there is born in you the ambition to reach the throne. There-
> fore you'll sing the beginning of this *duettino* sotto voce, and
> be sure that you give real importance to the lines, *Ma perché
> sento / rizzarsi il crine*. Pay attention to the indications, the
> accents, and to the *pp*'s and *f*'s marked in the music. (M 30)

But if Macbetto recoiled from what was making his hair rise,
he now recoils from that recoil, nobly resolving to "do the right
thing." To a broad new legato tune, rising and swelling, he sings
in full voice (*à voce aperta*, as opposed to the preceding *cupa*):

> Alla corona che m'offre il fato,
> La man rapace non alzerò, non alzerò.
> [To the crown extended me by fate
> A snatching hand I'll never raise, I'll never raise.]

This sounds noble, but the music undercuts the words. After
the surging first line, there is a drop to *pp* on the words "A snatching hand," and there are vertical accents over *non alzerò*, for soft
punches on them, as if Macbetto is reluctantly withholding his
hand. Then there is a crescendo up to a high F on the words "to me

by FATE." He is more proclaiming his destiny than refusing it. The note of triumph underscores that it *is* his fate, however he claims he will not grasp it. (How does one exempt oneself from fate?)

At this point Banco begins his musing, with short probing phrases: "How he is being filled with pride." Then Banco gives a rendition of Banquo's words in Shakespeare:

And oftentimes, to win us to our harm,
The instruments of darkness tell us truths,
Win us with honest trifles, to betray 's
In deepest consequence. (1.3.123–26)

While Banco is mulling this in reflective words (as if reluctant to think evil of his comrade), Macbetto repeats disjunct phrases from his preceding lines ("Two predictions . . . extended by fate"). Then, when Banco has finished his musing, Macbetto launches again into his blustery question, *"Ma perché sento,"* only this time instead of Macbetto trailing off timorously into the description of his hair rising, Banco sings in the same notes his own concern that Macbetto "is being filled with pride." Macbetto has fought down his first symptoms of fear, and passed the real worry on to Banco. As Macbetto repeats his claim that he will not raise a snatching hand to the crown and Banco patters against his claim, Macbetto ends the *duettino* with the surging line "My hand I'll never raise, I'll never raise, I'll never [crescendo mark from E to F] RAISE." While he says he will never raise it, the music rises in triumphal mode. Macbetto is like Peter Sellers in *Dr. Strangelove,* whose arm goes up in salute involuntarily.

Verdi labored over every detail of this "little duet," since he knew he had achieved a psychological breakthrough with it. We see the inner self of Macbetto as in an X-ray, a musical diagnosis. Though Macbetto takes the musical lead in this interchange, Banco is necessary as a symbol of the outer world Macbetto is already sealing out. Banco's failure to reach Macbetto shows how immediately he has plunged within himself, to begin the inner war that will shatter him.

THE MURDER

After Duncano arrives at Macbetto's castle in a dumb-show pageant of royal symbols, Macbetto is left alone still struggling with his temptation to murder. A plodding musical figure is cut off in midmeasure as Macbetto sees a dagger before him. Over rapid changes in the music, Macbetto shows that he is still divided. Macbetto both reaches for the dagger and recoils from it. He knows it is pointing where he wants to go—sweeping processional music carries Macbetto along as if inevitably. It begins with a hollow sound, as soft as can be ("*cupo, più piano che sia possibile*"), and gradually swells, along with Macbetto's voice, as he surrenders to his fate. But he goes forward with a divided self. After crying aloud at the knife's terrifying vision ("*orrenda immago*"), he describes the blood on it, his voice rising to a sweetly crooned high note, "with blood-spot it is *mo-ois*tened" (*la tua lama IR-RIga*). After some eerie night music—appropriate, he says, for witches to be performing their rites—he at last proclaims Duncano's death (in an expanding voice, *a voce spiegata*) and goes to effect it. Verdi's instruction to Varesi on this scene was:

> The first lines of the recitative—when he gives the orders to the servant—should be said without emphasis. But after he's

left alone, little by little he gets carried away, and he thinks he sees a dagger in his hands [*sic*], pointing the way to the murder of Duncan. This is a most beautiful moment, both dramatically and poetically, and you must take great care with it. (M 31)

After Macbetto returns from killing Duncano, his greatest duet with his wife takes place. This is this scene Verdi rehearsed over and over, and it was the piece most encored in the early days. Verdi said this and the sleepwalking scene were the keys to the whole opera. If they failed, the opera would fall. The churning music shows the turmoil of guilt locking Macbetto deeper into himself. He is in a place his wife cannot reach, as we see from the quite different music Verdi gives the two.

Earlier, Macbetto and Banco had mused past each other in their *duettino*. Now Macbetto and his wife whisper past each other with baffled insistence on their separate concerns. Her voice dances around his self-immurement, making little pickax chips at it, unable to break him out from his terrified dwelling on what he has done. The tense sung whispers are described by Verdi to Varesi (who is the central figure here):

Note that it is night, everyone is asleep, and the whole duet will have to be sung sotto voce, but in a hollow voice such as to arouse terror. Macbeth alone (as if momentarily transported) will sing a few phrases in full expansive voice. But all of this you will see explained in the piece. For you to understand my ideas clearly, let me tell you that in the entire recitative and duet, the orchestra consists of muted strings, two bassoons, two horns and a kettledrum. You see, the orchestra will play extremely softly, and therefore you will have to sing with mutes too. I urge you to bring out strongly the following poetic ideas, which are extremely beautiful.

> Ah, this hand,
> The Ocean could not
> Wash these hands of mine

And then

> Like angels of wrath, I shall hear
> Duncan's holy virtues thundering vengeance.

. . . at the end one should only barely-barely hear the words while Macbeth (almost beside himself) is dragged off by Lady. (M 31)

Giorgio Strehler said these are the detailed instructions that prove Verdi was a great director:

This musical and dramatic definition of the vocal texture is to all intents and purposes a directorial concept which illuminates the relationship of Macbeth and Lady Macbeth and goes straight to the heart of the psychological confusion of the two characters. This is how he was able to give expression to Shakespeare's idea and to his own.[5]

The best conveyers of a terrified secrecy in this exchange were, I think, the principals in the first *Macbeth* I ever saw, at the Met in 1959—Leonard Warren and Leonie Rysanek, under Erich Leinsdorf. Luckily, their performance was caught on record. Warren begins in the "hollow" voice that suggests whispering.

The two talk at cross-purposes about noises each heard. Lady asks him what he just said, and he is too distracted to remember. After a threefold cry of "Terrifying sight" (*Vista orribile*), Macbetto, in a daze, sings a sweet tune on his effort to say amen to the grooms' prayers—he cannot pray. Then he hears voices hammering in his head saying he will not sleep. The voices say that Glamis will not sleep, and Cawdor will not sleep. She mockingly uses the same titles to say that Glamis is stalled (*"t'arresti"*) and Cawdor is a silly boy (*"fanciul vanitoso"*). He is not paying any attention to her.

She sees he has absentmindedly carried away the dagger that is evidence of the crime. She grabs it and rushes to return, while he sings that the ocean cannot cleanse his hands. When she returns, she starts one of those Verdian delicate gallops that mean "Let's get out of here." He repeats the tune, fragmentarily, but while babbling still of his crime. Unable to recruit him, she just drags him away from the knocking at the gate.

From this point on, Macbetto rages in bafflement against his fate and his guilt—first at the banquet in Act 2, screaming at the ghost of Banco. Macbetto, out of guilt, sees the ghost, but no one else does. How do you stage that? Sometimes the ghost comes up from the trapdoor while the diners are looking elsewhere. Sometimes he shimmers behind scrims or is set off by weird lighting that the banqueters are not supposed to see. Shakespeare and Verdi make it clear that the actor playing Banquo should reappear, but spectrally. As Arthur Quiller-Couch put it:

Who sees the ghost? Not the company. Not even Lady Macbeth. Those who see it are Macbeth and you and I. Those into whom it strikes terror . . . those whom it accuses are

Macbeth and you and I. And what it accuses is what, of Macbeth, you and I are hiding in our breasts.

I have never observed or heard of this scene being so convincingly enacted as in the 2010 Chicago Lyric Opera production directed by Barbara Gaines. Here Thomas Hampson, the veteran and superb Macbetto, leaped athletically onto the banquet table, on the end slanting toward the audience, and sang his strutting welcome to the guests. But the huge cylindrical chandelier of multicolored glass panels and jangling beads, which had commanded the scene from our first sight of it, suddenly opened just behind Hampson, and the bloody ghost leaned out of it and grabbed his shoulders, making him open his arms in a crucifixion terror. The audience was as surprised and horrified as Macbetto, the effect which was always intended and never quite realized in the past. Lady, who tried to shake him out of his terror, tugged on his cloak from beside the table, not seeing what he felt and we (alone) saw.

In the last act, Macbetto's growing fatalism gives him a numbness to all feeling. First he sings of giving up any hope of love or reputation. Then, told of his wife's death, he gives Shakespeare's "tale told by an idiot" speech (5.5.17–28). Verdi wrote to Varesi:

There is an adagio in D flat, every detail of which needs coloring, cantabile and *affettuoso*. As for the lines to the intervening passage,

Life, what does it mean?
'Tis a tale told by a poor idiot
Wind and sound signifying nothing.

I want you to declaim them with all the irony and contempt possible. (M 41)

In the course of the opera Lady becomes a witch. Now Macbetto has become a blaspheming nihilist. His "Life is nothing" matches Jago's *"La morte è il nulla."* Macbetto's soul is destroyed along with his body, without even the hint of redemption that comes to Lady in her sleepwalking agitation. In the end, Macbetto has no feeling, while Lady has too much feeling—it shakes her entirely apart. Macbetto was crushed at once by guilt, but he shrugs it doggedly off. Guilt eats more stealthily at his Lady, and does not eat everything away.

Notes

1. Orson Welles in his movie of *Macbeth* shows that he does not understand the isolation of the two main characters, who have not been together for two acts, when he has Macbeth show up at the sleepwalking scene and lead his wife to bed.
2. For old views of the faint-or-feint controversy see the New Variorium *Macbeth,* edited by H. H. Furness (Dover, 1963), pp. 161–64. For the difficulty of acting the feint, see Marvin Rosenberg, *The Masks of Macbeth* (University of Delaware Press, 1978), pp. 174–78.
3. Rosenberg, op. cit., p. 176.
4. W. H. Auden, *Lectures on Shakespeare* (Princeton University Press, 2000), pp. 211–12.
5. Giorgio Strehler, *Corriere d'Informazione,* November 1, 1973.

4
Lady

It has often been said or written that Lady is the most important character in Verdi's opera. That is certainly not true in the number of lines she sings—any more than it is in Shakespeare's play, where Macbeth speaks 725 lines to his wife's 263. More important, Verdi's Lady does not, for some time, show the inner complexity that his Macbetto does. Until the sleepwalking scene, her brief reappearance in the last act, we have little reason to think she has been in anguish. Shakespeare's earlier hints of this are omitted. In Verdi, she does not faint and get carried out in the discovery-of-murder scene. She does not say, "It will make *us* mad."

Most significant of all, in the play it is Macbeth who decides on Banquo's murder—he tells her, "Be innocent of the knowledge, dearest chuck" (3.2.45). But Verdi makes her prod Macbetto to the deed. Verdi expressly told his librettist to make her the prime mover in Banco's death, and writes "the assassins come on to carry out *Lady's* orders" (M 13). In Shakespeare, she does not know beforehand about the murder of Lady Macduff and her children. In Verdi, she cheers him on to it in an odd vendetta song. Of the banquet scene, Verdi wrote: "The important character, the dominating demon of this scene, is Lady, and however much Macbetto can distinguish himself as an actor, Lady, I repeat, dominates and controls everything" (M 99). In the 1987

Claude d'Anna production on DVD, Leo Nucci plays his role at first like a puzzled bull, responding to the picadorlike goadings of Shirley Verrett as Lady. This is very true to Verdi's conception.

Thus, in the opera, Lady is an unrelieved harridan and villainous in all her early scenes. Admittedly, she is a grandly impressive villainess. At her first appearance, in Act 1, she enters reading the letter from Macbetto. Barbieri-Nini wanted a grander entry, but Maria Callas proved that the reading itself can be dramatic. She begins matter-of-factly, as if this were any letter, then raises her voice to emphasize *"Sir di Caudore."* After a hesitation as if taking in what this could mean, she proceeds, but hesitates again after "predicted" to go on, wonderingly, at "a garland for my head." After finishing the letter, she launches into a triumphant cry (*"grandioso"* is the marking): *"Ambizioso spirito"* (Ambitious drive), and for a second we might think she is declaring her own driving spirit. But then she drops her voice and says, " . . . you have, Macbeth." She doubts that his ambition is marked by a corresponding and necessary will to wickedness: "The path to power is filled with crimes, and unhappy the one who puts a timorous foot on it before drawing back." Already she has defined the difference between them. Hers is the force that does not hesitate at crime.

Though she doubts that he is up to the crimes she foresees, she sets to work curing him of virtue. Her first aria begins "Come! Hurry!" In a surging aria that leaps high and dives low, she flexes her muscles in song. She repeats, "What holds you? What holds you? What holds you?" (*Che tardi? Che tardi? Che tardi?*). Such threefold repetitions are characteristic of her impatient nagging. Verdi told Barbieri-Nini to make the pleas urgent:

I would ask you to consider carefully the phrase at the words

Che tardi? Accetta il dono,
Ascendivi a regnar.
[What holds you? Take what's given,
Rise up to reign.]

and do it in such a way that the voice does not swell up all at once, but gradually; and to give meaningful emphasis each time to the words *Che tardi*. (M 29)

Lady at the third *"Che tardi?"* sings of the rise toward the crown with repeated climbings of the voice, "rise up to *reign*, rise up to *REIGN*." After her aria, a messenger tells her that the king is coming to her castle, and she cannot believe her luck. She repeats "Here?" (*Qui?*), first inquisitively, as if it is just dawning on her what this could lead to, then confirmingly, as if moving to her conclusion from the inquisitiveness, then triumphant with resolve on what she will do *"here."* Verdi instructed Barbieri:

In the passage that comes before the cabaletta, pay careful attention to the words *qui . . . qui . . . la notte*. These words have tremendous significance; in short, they should arouse applause. (M 29)

The cabaletta, the climactic sequel to an aria, darkly summons the infernal spirits, then rises by their inspiration to the heights of murder. Verdi said of this:

The first part of the cabaletta is to be pronounced in a grandiose manner, with pride, but mingled with the pride there should be joy. In the second part, the phrase at the words *Tu notte ne avvolgi* [You, Night, wrap me round] etc. will perhaps be low; but it is precisely my intention to make it dark and mysterious . . . so then to have all the brilliance at the end. (M 29)

When Macbetto comes to his wife, and she says the king should not leave their house, Callas positively leers the second syllable of her question, *"Inte-endi?"* (You fo-ollow me?). Macbetto first answers faintly as if trying to summon resolve: *"Intendo"* (I follow), then as if playing catch-up to her macho: *"INTENDO"* (I FOLLOW). The king arrives, though he has not a line to sing. In Shakespeare, the king is a powerful presence on the battlefield and in his arrival at the castle. Verdi, having excised the battle-field scene and cut the castle arrival, felt that a singer could not be sufficiently royal in a walk-on part to make his murder a political disaster, so he let a royal pageant serve as the king's symbolic arrival. (Claude d'Anna, in his movie, had a curtained carriage bring in the king, from which his gloved hand, thrust through the curtain, is held for Macbetto to kiss—when the carriage goes out after the murder, the same hand flops out of the curtain with blood on it.)

When the murder is discovered and the whole court assembles to express its horror, Verdi interrupts this outburst with a heartfelt prayer sung a cappella, for which Verdi instructed Varesi, "You and Barbieri will have to be very accurate to keep the others [on pitch]" (M 31). The finale is what Budden calls one of Verdi's "groundswells" (B 1.170), but which I prefer to think of as Verdi's Great Wheel—where, over a propulsive accompanying pattern, choral surges rise, cross each other, change harmonies, and keep mounting, mounting. Once he sets the Great Wheel going, it has tremendous power.

In Act 2, Verdi added a magnificent aria for Lady in his 1865 revision of the work for Paris. He gives her Macbeth's words "Light thickens" as *"La luce langue"* (Light falters). Over a sinuously warbling figure, she imbibes the soft, insidious darkness, setting her mood for the chilling outburst "More crime—we need it, WE NEED IT!" (*Nuovo delitto—è necessario, È NECESSARIO!*). Then she chortles over her reward for crime, the throne: "O voluptuous throne! O scepter!" Over these words Verdi put in the score: "In a tiny voice, slightly pulsing" (*con voce pianissimo, un po oscillante*). He explained for Paris what he meant by *oscillante:*

> I want a *mezza voce,* and as soft as possible, but it should be one with resonance in it, not robotic (*ventriloca*). Pulsing (*oscillante*) to express joy, but it should not be too tremulous, which would sound feverish. In short, express the words and there it is (*voilà tout*). (M 84)

At the banquet, Lady sings the drinking song (*brindisi*), a jerky, spiky tune with many trills (the one thing Callas could not do). It suggests an appropriately brittle gaiety in an uneasy court, and the willpower of Lady is shown when, after the grisly interruptions as Macbetto screams at a ghost invisible to everyone else, she gamely repeats the *brindisi*. Good singing actresses show what an effort this is, and the spasmodic line lets them do it. An early marked score notes that one Lady "delivered the reprise of the *brindisi* with an emphatic break after each of the two first lines, as if Lady were having to summon all her power to continue the song" (M 365). Verdi was right to say that the Paris production should not let Macduffo, instead of Lady, repeat the song (M 93)—though Paris did it anyway.

After Macbetto consults the witches in Act 3, he immediately, with no scene change, meets Lady—where? This is a rather uncomfortable addition to Shakespeare, done apparently just to give Lady more to sing. How did she get to the witches' lair, or he back to the castle? He begins to tell her what the witches revealed. At each bit of news she repeats impatiently, as is her wont, "And? . . . And? . . . And?" (*Segui . . . Segui . . . Segui*). When he says the witches told him that Banco's heirs will reign, she repeats defiantly "A lie! A lie! A lie!" (*Menzogna! Menzogna! Menzogna!*) and urges Macbetto to kill them all. They launch into a typical vengeance song. *Vendetta! Vendetta! Vendetta!* (Whom are they avenging? The ones who need to suffer revenge for wrong are themselves.)

Since in the opera we are not going to see Macduff's son killed, the scene shifts in Act 4 to the English border, to express the sufferings of Scotland under Macbetto. Verdi loved to write exile choruses, to repeat his first great success with one, "Va, pensiero," in *Nabucco*. This is a particularly beautiful example, with a gentle religious tone, and it prepares the way for Macduffo's one aria, "Ah, la paterna mano." I noted earlier that we seldom if ever get to hear a star tenor sing this in the house, but we do have the towering recording of it made by Caruso in 1916. He begins the recitative with a plangent cry, "Oh sons, oh sons of mine, killed with your hapless mother!" Then his voice swells with anger at himself: "I left in that tiger's claws the mother"—and he ends with a swooning tenderness—"and sons."

The aria begins, Verdi marks, sweetly ("*dolce*"): "A father's hand did not shield you, dear ones, from the faithless butchers who felled you in death." Then a timorous confession, marked "*pp dolce*," with the melancholy coloring Caruso could give his voice: "On me in flight, in hiding"—each syllable now accented— "you / called, / you / called—in vain"—now tearful—"with your last sobbing, with your last, with your last breathing." Another change in coloring, now to fierceness, voice rising like a rocket: "Bring me before the tyrant, Lord God, and if he slips my grasp you may embrace him with your pardon." Verdi, a little wistfully, wished that the first production of the opera had a better tenor for this aria, "which, if it were sung by, say [Carlo] Guasco, would cause a furor" (M 35). No one, not even Guasco, could equal what Caruso does with this song.[1]

Now comes the sleepwalking, where all of Lady's ferocity is melted into regretful longings and bitter loss. Earlier, when Macbetto was sealed up in guilt, muttering to himself, Lady tried to break through his wall of self-imprisonment. There is no one to make a similar effort at reaching her as she broods in a terrible isolation. The asymmetric arcs of Macbetto and his wife are complete, with him frozen in numb denial, and her subconsciously confessing her crimes. If she, with her taper and gown and bare feet, is undergoing the punishment of a witch, it is the garb of a *repenting* witch, the kind for which there was still enough hope to avoid being hanged.

Verdi had avoided the stock mad scenes of Donizetti and Bellini. Here he plays a clever variation on that theme. A standard device of their mad scenes was the playing of music from earlier parts of the opera, sad or glad, as the deranged woman remembers the past. Verdi composes all new music here, in highly original form, fragmented but with a unity of feeling. It is true that the introduction to the opera had themes from the sleepwalking, but that was a borrowing in reverse, with sleepwalking the source and the introduction the echo.

It was noted earlier that Barbieri, with Verdi's encouragement, observed an actual sleepwalker. So did Mrs. Siddons.[2] One may wonder how, if the singer is carrying a taper, she can make the hand-washing gestures. She must put the taper down, in its candle-holder, on some handy table. Mrs. Siddons did that, then mimed pouring water from an invisible pitcher.[3] On Shakespeare's open stage, with no furniture, John Rice must have put the taper, for a time, on the floor. Verdi leaves no doubt in the matter. Before she starts rubbing her hands, the score indicates that "Lady *puts down the light* and rubs her hands as if to get rid of something" (L 2.541).

Verdi's concern over the details of this scene is clear from what he wrote ahead for the Paris production:

And so we come to the sleepwalking scene, which is always the high point of the opera. Anyone who has seen [Adelaide] Ristori [in Shakespeare's play] knows that it should be done with only the most sparing gestures, even being limited to perhaps a single gesture, that of wiping out a bloodstain that she thinks she has on her hand. The movements should be slow, and one should not see her taking steps; her feet should glide over the ground as if she were a statue or a ghost walking. The eyes fixed, the appearance corpse-like, she is in agony, and dies soon after. Ristori employed a rattle in her throat, the death rattle.[4] In music that cannot and must not be done, just as one should not cough in the last act of *La Traviata,* or laugh in the "Scherzo od è follia" of *Ballo in Maschera.* Here there is an English horn lament that takes the place of the death-rattle perfectly well and more poetically. The piece should be sung with the utmost simplicity and *voce cupa* (she is dying) but without ever letting the voice become robotic (*ventriloca*). There are some moments in which the voice can open up, but they must be brief flashes, as indicated in the score. In sum, for the effect and the terror that this number should inspire, one needs a *corpse-like appearance, voce cupa, espressivo*, etc.

Note too that here, as much as in the Act I duet, if the singers do not sing sotto voce the result will be disagreeable, because there is too much disproportion, too much imbalance, between the singers and the orchestra—the orchestra has only a few instruments and the violins are muted. (M 110–11)

Verdi wanted to stay particularly close to Shakespeare in this crucial scene. Dissatisfied with Piave's effort, he called on his friend Andrea Maffei—"Saint Andrew to the rescue" (M 34)—to get the Italian prose lines closer to Shakespeare's "mad" prose. Under the lyric fragments crafted by Maffei, Verdi weaves a hushed musical spell, instructing the singers "sotto voce throughout" (L 2.542). An upward chromatic thrust on the muted strings depicts Lady's hard scrubbing at the "damned spot" (*macchia*) on her hand. This had occurred in the opera's orchestral introduction, where it seemed just a punctuation point in the melody. Only when we see it explained by Lady's stage action do we realize how appropriate it was to an opera devoted to the subject of murder and guilt.

In standard mad scenes, Shakespeare has the crazed one or a fool sing snatches of ballads or old songs. Ophelia sings obscene snatches to show her sexual frustration. Shakespeare has Lady Macbeth sing a Scottish ballad with particular meaning, "The Thane of Fife had a wife; where is she now?" (5.1.42–43).

Shakespeare had given the sole responsibility for Lady Macduff's murder to Macbeth. That Lady Macbeth sings about Macduff's wife in her sleepwalking shows that she has learned about the murder, and mixes it in with her guilty memories of Duncan's death. Verdi, by contrast, makes Lady the instigator of all the opera's murders, and shows her repenting them in her sleep. Maffei, to give the singer a chance to dwell more on the murder of Macduffo's wife, expands a bit: "The Thane of Fife—husband and father was he not? But now? What became of him?"

Where Shakespeare wrote, "Yet who would have thought the old man to have had so much blood in him?" (5.1.39–40), Maffei shifted the "think" element to the end, so Verdi could repeat the emphatic word as Lady dwells on the image—"*tanto sangue immaginar, IMMAGINAR, immaginar.*" Lady ends by urging Macbetto to come away, just as she had at the end of the great Act 1 duet. But where she had whispered a sprightly gallop in the first scene, she goes through slow-motion dragging in her sleep. Verdi marks it "simply and slow in cadence" (L 2.525). As Verdi said, he lets the English horn do the "weeping" for Lady, who is not to sob or gasp. But Callas conveys anguish by the low chest notes Verdi gives her—which makes all the more striking the high D-flat at the end, which Verdi calls "a [mere] thread of sound" (L 2.555). It is as if her soul were evaporating into the night sky.

Notes

1. Guasco had sung the leading tenor roles in Verdi's *I Lombardi, Ernani,* and *Attila.*
2. Sarah Siddons, "Remarks on the Character of Lady Macbeth," in Thomas Campbell, *The Life of Mrs. Siddons* (E. Wilson, 1834), vol. 2, pp. 38–39.

3. Ibid., pp. 37–40. Mrs. Siddons had put down the taper in her performances outside of London, and the dramatist Richard Brinsley Sheridan came backstage to tell her she must not do that in London, where famous actresses had not done so. She said it was absurd to think of washing one's hands with a taper in one of them.

4. Verdi seems to have misunderstood Ristori's labored breathing at one point. Shakespeare's line "'Here's the smell of the blood,'" she said, "caused me to breathe with difficulty" (M 363).

Otello

II

5

Rossini's *Otello*

When Verdi, in the late 1870s, began to consider setting Shakespeare's *Othello* as an opera, he faced an obstacle that has faded now but was still very much in his way at the time. His most important predecessor in Italian opera, Gioacchino Rossini, had set the Othello story half a century earlier, and it was still being performed. Rossini's work had been a great success, and continued to be a potential rival. Between its premiere in 1816 and 1890, there were over 290 productions of it in eighty-seven cities in twenty-four countries, including translations into eight languages.[1] Its original singers added to their already great fame with this box-office hit. The painter Delacroix used Rossini's opera, not Shakespeare's play, as the basis for an ambitious series of prints and paintings of the Othello story.[2] Giacomo Meyerbeer attended a Venetian performance of *Otello* in 1818 and wrote to his brother:

> [The third act] elicited a furor the like of which has not been heard in twenty years, and which was so great that after thirty performances, all sold out, the enthusiasm was so enormous that [Nicola] Tacchinardi and [Francesca] Festa were granted very large sums to play a continuous three-month run this coming autumn.[3]

Herbert Weinstock rightly says: "The gigantic Verdian *Otello* has made the onetime universal popularity of Rossini's opera all but incredible to some twentieth-century operagoers."[4] No one doubted the power of the opera in the nineteenth century.

It is true that Rossini's work met some early and severe criticism, but that came from the few people in Italy who knew Shakespeare's play, and they had the misapprehension that Rossini used (and abused) it. Lord Byron, for instance, wrote from Venice: "They have been crucifying *Othello* into an opera . . . the greatest nonsense . . . the handkerchief turned into a *billet doux*" (O 765). But neither Rossini nor his librettist knew the English drama. They were setting a French variant on the story. If one takes that into account, the criticisms of the learned fall by the way. As Philip Gossett put it:

> Had the principal characters of the opera . . . been named Enrico, Zenobia, and Ricciardo, instead of Otello, Desdemona, and Rodrigo, few spectators would have imagined that the first two acts had anything whatsoever to do with Shakespeare's *Othello*. Instead, they would have rightly perceived that the opera explores certain archetypical situations of contemporary Italian opera.[5]

Rossini was working from a libretto written by a fashionable nobleman, the Marchese Francesco Maria Berio di Salsa. Stendhal, the early biographer of Rossini, had frequented Berio's salon in Naples, and described him as "a man who is as charming a companion in society as he is unfortunate and abominable as a poet."[6]

Berio, according to Stendhal, completely botched the story. In his version, Desdemona's father has destined her to marry Rodrigo. When she reveals that she is already secretly married to Otello, her father curses her. Otello, chancing on the scene, thinks she is in fact about to abandon him for Rodrigo. It is easy to see why those who knew Shakespeare's story would think this was a mess.

But Verdi's librettist, the composer-intellectual Arrigo Boito, could learn certain things from Rossini's earlier attempt to make an opera of the tale. To begin with, all operas taken from plays (or, for that matter, from novels) have to cut them drastically. Song lingers over characters' thoughts or encounters in ways that slow the progress of the story. In the case of *Othello*, the double location—beginning in Venice, then moving to Cyprus—not only violates the classical unity of place but complicates the story and multiplies scenes and sets. Berio eliminated Cyprus, as Boito would eliminate Venice. Both librettists open with Otello arriving fresh from a victory over the Turks—he returns to Venice in Berio's script; he reaches Cyprus in Boito's. Berio drops Cassio entirely, making Rodrigo the only love rival for Otello.

It was earlier noticed that four of the five male singers in Rossini are tenors. The composer compensates for this uniformity by a careful adjustment of timbre among the male leads. The part of Otello he gave to Andrea Nozzari, whose voice had more heft than that of Giovanni David, who played Rodrigo as a florid high tenor. Yet Nozzari's was a purer tenor than the baritonal tenor of Giuseppe Ciccimarra, who played Iago. Nozzari was not only vocally but visually contrasted with his fellow cast members. Stendhal described his performance as Otello with special fondness:

> His magnificent stature, which could convey so stirringly an impression of grandeur tinged with melancholy, was extremely valuable to him in expressing certain aspects of

the role, and interpreting conceptions of which the librettist had probably never dreamed. I well remember the astonishment with which the Neapolitan audience reacted to the pure beauty of his gestures, and to the general impression of rare and graceful majesty which was characteristic of Nozzari in the part. Incidentally, the style of his acting on this occasion was quite outside his usual repertoire.[7]

Rossini's way of pitting voices of different timbre against each other resulted, in Otello, in what Stendhal called "the glorious rivalry" of Nozzari and David as Otello and Rodrigo, "striving to outdo each other in perfection, goaded higher and ever higher in achievement by the spurs of emulation."[8]

Rossini brought to Otello a new dramaturgy. He gave it a simpler dignity than was manifested in his earlier works. For the first time he accompanied the recitative with full orchestra, and he retained the tragic ending of the story, though it was the fashion to give happy endings to Shakespeare's tragedies. (Later, a happy ending would be substituted for Rossini's original.) Though Byron and Stendhal damned the Otello libretto, both of them admired the music—and with good cause. Stendhal was swept away by the great Giuditta Pasta singing Desdemona's arias in Paris. The architectonics of the first-act finale are ingenious. The chorus sings a wedding song of concord, but the trio that follows is a widely spaced one where all three singers misunderstand each other—Desdemona tries to let her father and Rodrigo know she cannot marry, for she is already married, but they continue to ignore her efforts. Then Otello enters and misunderstands all the other misunderstandings. By these interjections the chorus's first joyous song is turned into one of shock and hate.

In the second act, Iago misrepresents a letter from Desdemona to Otello as if it were intended for Rodrigo. Otello reads out lines from the letter, interjecting cries of anguish while Iago mutters his glee—a scene that resembles Verdi's in Act 3 where Otello reads the letter from Venice's ruler, interjecting his own outbursts. Above all, Rossini's third act created a rapturous response by its dramatic force. Here the tale is very close to Shakespeare's final act (except that Otello stabs Desdemona rather than smothers her). Desdemona sings her "Willow Song," upset and interrupted by a storm, and utters a prayer. Meyerbeer wrote of a Venetian performance:

> The third act of *Otello* established its reputation so firmly that a thousand blunders could not shake it. This third act is really godlike, and what is so extraordinary is that its beauties are absolutely anti-Rossinian. First-rate declamation, ever-impassioned recitative, mysterious accompaniment full of local color, and, in particular, the style of the old-time romances at its highest perfection.[9]

It was Rossini's own idea to have Desdemona hear a gondolier passing along a canal as he sings a sad song. The composer told the librettist that the song's words must be Francesca's in Dante's *Inferno* (5.121–23): "No greater pain than to remember in one's misery a happier time." Berio said no Venetian gondolier would know the Florentine poet, but Rossini said the words must be used, since they fit Desdemona's mood precisely. Liszt transcribed the gondolier's song in the second movement of his *Venezia e Napoli* (B 3.304).

There is a long orchestral introduction to Otello's entry into the bedchamber. One wonders why it takes so long for Otello to approach the sleeping Desdemona. Stendhal explains how the drama was heightened in Naples:

During this *ritornello,* far away in the uttermost depths of the stage, and incredibly distant, we glimpse Otello, a lantern held high in his hand, and his naked *cangiar* under his arm, tip-toeing towards his wife's chamber, down the winding staircase of a tower. This stairway, which winds downward in a spiral, gives us glimpses of the fearful visage of Otello, a lonely point of light picked out by the lantern in the midst of this infinite ocean of darkness, appearing, disappearing, and then appearing again as he follows the twists of the little stairway, which is his only path. Now and then, the light catches the blade of the unsheathed *cangiar,* and the gleam of steel flashes a chill warning of the coming murder. After an infinite length of time, Otello reaches the front of the stage, moves across to the bed, and parts the curtains. At this climax, no description would be anything but a superfluous piece of impertinence. Let it be enough simply to recall the magnificent stature of Nozzari, and his profoundly moving acting. Otello sets down his lantern, a gust of wind blows it out. He hears Desdemona cry out in her sleep, *Amato ben.* Flashes of lightning chase each other now across the sky in an ever-quickening succession, as in some southern storm, and their light flickers into the fateful chamber.[10]

If Stendhal gives us the scenic power of the last act, Philip Gossett best describes its musical texture:

The act is conceived as a musical entity, and although one can identify the gondoliere's canzone, the willow song and prayer, the duet, and the final catastrophe, none is truly independent. Desdemona's willow song is ostensibly strophic, but Rossini's handling of vocal ornamentation gives it a more sophisticated structure. The first strophe is simple, a beautiful harp-accompanied melody. The second is more ornamented, and the third is quite florid. But the storm brews without and within, and when, after a short section of arioso from the frightened Desdemona, she begins the final strophe, it is utterly barren of any ornament. Finally, unable to finish, she trails off into arioso. Although the first section of the Otello-Desdemona duet is traditional, its ending, which builds in intensity until Otello kills Desdemona, is not. There is no room for a cabaletta, and Rossini offers none, though the text had been fashioned to suggest the typical cabaletta structure. Throughout the act, the drama is the controlling element, and the music, while never abdicating its own rights, reinforces it. In Act 3 of *Otello*, Rossini came of age as a musical dramatist.[11]

Though Verdi would overwhelm Rossini's *Otello* with his own, the challenge offered by the older master was no negligible one. As Julian Budden saw, Rossini's last act, with its gondolier's song, "remained like a sentinel barring the way to any composer rash enough to attempt a subject that Rossini was considered to have made his own" (B 3.304). Verdi knew he had his work cut out for him when he took on such a great preceding work. To the idea that he was being presumptuous in giving his new opera the same title as Rossini's (instead of calling it, say, *Jago*), Verdi told his librettist, Boito, "I prefer it if they say, 'He tried to fight a giant and was crushed,' rather than, 'He tried to hide behind the title of Jago'" (O 200).

Notes

1. Roberta Montemorra Marvin, "Shakespeare and *Primo Ottocento* Italian Opera: The Case of Rossini's *Otello*," in *The Opera and Shakespeare*, edited by Holger Klein and Christopher Smith (Edwin Mellen Press, 1994), p. 71.
2. Ibid., p. 90.
3. Meyerbeer quoted in Herbert Weinstock, *Rossini* (Alfred A. Knopf, 1968), p. 69.
4. Ibid.
5. Philip Gossett, "Introduction," in *Early Romantic Opera*, edited by Philip Gossett and Charles Rosen (Garland Press, 1978), p. 1.
6. Stendhal, *Life of Rossini*, translated by Richard N. Coe (Orion Press, 1970), p. 233.
7. Ibid., p. 221.
8. Ibid., p. 226.
9. Meyerbeer quoted in Weinstock, op. cit., p. 69.
10. Stendhal, op. cit., pp. 234–35.
11. Philip Gossett, in *The New Grove Masters of Italian Opera* (W. W. Norton, 1983), pp. 35–37.

6

Boito

Verdi had a great advantage over Rossini's *Otello* (1816) in composing his own *Otello* (1887). It was an advantage, even, over Verdi's
own earlier Shakespearean work, *Macbeth*. By the 1880s he had as
his librettist Arrigo Boito, a highly cultured poet and musician, a
man as serious about getting to the true meaning of Shakespeare
as was Verdi himself. Besides the two works Boito created with
Verdi (*Otello* and *Falstaff*), he wrote a libretto for *Hamlet*, to be
composed by his friend and fellow musician Franco Faccio. He
also translated and condensed *Antony and Cleopatra*, for performance by his lover, the great Italian actress Eleonora Duse.

The later collaboration between Verdi and Boito could not
have been expected from their early contacts, which had created
enmity between them. Boito came from a talented and aristocratic family. His father, Silvestro, was a painter of miniatures for
Gregory XVI in the Vatican (O 811–12). His mother was a Polish
countess. His older brother Camillo was an architect, historian,
and novelist, for forty-five years the professor of architecture
at the Brera Academy of Fine Arts in Milan. Arrigo shared his
brother's wide culture and high aspirations as a theorist of the
arts. Early on, the brothers were Scapigliati ("Raggedys"), members of the Milan circle of young writers, painters, and musicians
who scoffed at older Italian styles (including that of Verdi). The
Raggedys enjoyed a radical lifestyle, idolizing Baudelaire, com-
muning over hashish and absinthe. Some of them, including

their best-known poet, Emilio Praga, died young of alcoholism or suicide. One of the Scapigliati, Giuseppe Giacosa, remembered his young artistic days when he cowrote the libretto for Puccini's *La Bohème*. Clarina Maffei, who had the most famous and influential salon in Milan, welcomed the Scapigliati to her home, in what Tom Wolfe would later call an exercise in radical chic. This got her, temporarily, into trouble with her old friend Verdi.

Verdi had been close to Clarina's ex-husband, Andrea, the man who helped him with Piave's libretto for *Macbeth*. In 1862, drawing on her extensive Parisian connections, Clarina suggested to Verdi, who was in Paris at the time, that he get a text for his *Inno delle Nazioni* (to be sung at the International Exhibition in London) from the twenty-year-old Boito, who had just arrived in Paris. Verdi knew nothing of Boito at the time, but he was in a hurry to get the irksome London commission off his hands, so he accepted her suggestion. Only later did he become aware of what he considered the disturbing views of the Scapigliati, which made him deeply hostile to them.

Boito and Franco Faccio, as students at the Milan Conservatory, conceived the ambition of remaking Italian music, taking their inspiration from the north, from Mendelssohn and Meyerbeer and Wagner. They condemned the Italian opera of their day as more interested in formulas than in form.[1] They collaborated at the conservatory on two patriotic cantatas, *Il Quattro Giugno* (1860) and *Le Sorelle d'Italia* (1861). They graduated with prize money for travel abroad, which took Boito to Paris and the composition of Verdi's *Inno*. Back in Italy, Franco Faccio composed his first opera, *I Profughi Fiamminghi*, to a libretto by Emilio Praga, which received its debut at La Scala in 1863, when Faccio was only twenty-three. At a banquet honoring this event, Boito read

a boastful ode for his promising schoolmate, "All'Arte Italiana."
It contained lines that earned an ill fame:

> He may already be born
> who will raise again an art,
> chaste and severe, on the altar
> slimed like a brothel wall. (O xxx)

Unfortunately for all concerned, this brash poem was gos-
siped about, and printed in the *Museo di Famiglia*, where Verdi
read it and took it as an insult to his own body of work. In a
sarcastic letter to his publisher Tito Ricordi, he wrote: "If among
others I, too, have soiled the altar, as Boito says, let him clean it,
and I will be the first to light a little candle" (O xxx). Over and
over, for years, Verdi bitterly recalled the "slimed altar" line in
his letters. As Frank Walker says, "Was there ever a composer so
sensitive to criticism, so tenacious in rancor?"[2] It did not help that
Boito's music teacher and patron was Alberto Mazzucato, then
the principal conductor at La Scala, whom Verdi despised.

When Clarina Maffei persisted in promoting her young
friends to Verdi, he broke off relations with her, and his wife had
to scan incoming letters to intercept those that would anger him
by praising the upstarts.[3] Meanwhile, the upstarts kept starting up. In 1865, Faccio premiered his second opera, *Amleto*, to
Boito's libretto from Shakespeare. In the same year, Boito and
Praga launched their critical journal, *Il Figaro*, and Boito and Faccio joined Garibaldi's guerrilla fighters against the Austrians. In
1868, Boito conducted at La Scala the premiere of *Mefistofele*, for
which he was both librettist and composer as well as conductor.
It was a disastrous failure. Only seven years later, in a radically

altered form, did it achieve success, first at Bologna and then throughout Italy.

Faccio, meanwhile, had given up composing after the failure of his revised *Amleto* in 1871. He concentrated on conducting, since he was meeting with particular success at leading Verdi operas in Germany and Scandinavia—so much so that a softened Verdi chose him to conduct the Italian premiere of *Aida* in 1872. Boito, too, was doing less composing, though he continued to work, with dogged disappointment, on his second opera, never finished—*Nerone*. He continued to write librettos for other composers—for Coronaro's *Un Tramonto* (1873), Catalani's *La Falce* (1875), Ponchielli's *La Gioconda* (1876), San Germano's *Semira* (withdrawn in rehearsal), Carlos Gomes's *Maria Tudor* (1879, finishing a libretto by his late colleague Emilio Praga), Bottesini's *Ero e Leandro* (1879), Pick-Mangiagalli's *Basi e Bote* (1887, though not performed till 1927), Dominicetti's *Iram* (not composed).

But the life-changing work on which Boito's fame would rest began in 1879, when Giulio Ricordi got Verdi to start considering, slowly, a collaboration with Boito on *Otello*. Before that project could be truly launched, there was a trial run as Boito revised the libretto of Verdi's 1857 opera, *Simon Boccanegra*. The surviving Scapigliati, who had shed their youthful cheekiness, were gradually joining the circle of Verdi admirers. Ricordi, who was the same age as Boito and Faccio, had been a young musical theorist in their circle, but as he grew older he took on the responsibilities of his father Tito's publishing house and became a trusted business adviser to Verdi. He worked with the ever-diplomatic wife of Verdi, Giuseppina Strepponi, to coax Verdi into looking at Boito's libretto for Shakespeare's *Othello* (at this stage called *Jago*).

Mutual respect grew between them as they worked together on *Simon Boccanegra*.

Simon had not been a success at its premiere, but it has rich music and resonant political themes, and Verdi hoped to salvage the best parts of it. Ricordi kept urging him to revise it, though Verdi thought that *Aida* and the *Requiem Mass* would be his crowning (and final) works. He had grown to hate the endless battles that were involved in getting the right singers, conductors, and productions for his ever-more-demanding works. But Boito brought fresh eyes to the subject of *Simon Boccanegra*. He argued that the characters had to become more "living," the Council Scene more dramatic, the action more comprehensible. Verdi resisted sinking too much energy into large revisions, but Boito cajoled and suggested, reinvigorating the Maestro's creative force (B 2.256–61). The revised work, conducted by Faccio at La Scala, was a success in 1881. Victor Maurel (the future Jago) sang the role of Boccanegra, Francesco Tamagno (the future Otello) that of Gabriele. Thus was assembled the team (Verdi, Boito, Ricordi, Faccio, Tamagno, Maurel) that would triumph, six years later, at the premiere of *Otello*.

Verdi and Boito grew in affection for each other over the years of their collaboration. Verdi at first would not even let Ricordi bring Boito to visit him, since he feared a commitment to new work. But composer and librettist soon came to love and seek each other's company. In 1885, Boito was still writing him: "My desire to see you again is great, but my fear of disturbing you is equally great" (O 175). Verdi answered: "You could never disturb us! Come, and you will give great pleasure to me, and to Peppina, too" (O 176).

Nonetheless, dealing with Verdi was always a ticklish prospect. Anything could make him shy from a major undertaking in his seventies. When Boito's *Mefistofele* received a successful Naples production in 1884, he was given a celebratory banquet at which he spoke with enthusiasm about the *Otello* libretto he was working on. The newspaper *Il Piccolo* interpreted his words to mean that he wished he could compose the opera himself. Verdi read another report of the banquet in the Neapolitan paper *Il Pungolo,* and fired off a letter to Franco Faccio:

> I address myself to you, Boito's oldest, most steadfast friend, so that upon his return to Milan you may tell him in person, not in writing, that—without the shadow of resentment, without any deep-seated anger—I return his manuscript to him intact. Furthermore, since the libretto is my property, I offer it to him as a gift, for whenever he intends to compose it. If he accepts this I will be happy—happy in the hope of having furthered and served the art we all love. (O 154)

Faccio responded instantly that Boito had been misunderstood, and expressed "what he [Boito], I, Ricordi, and all who love and long for the glory of Italian art would feel if you really were to resolve not to write *Otello*" (O 155). Boito, when he heard what Verdi had written to Faccio, was shattered. He wrote a long and emotional letter telling Verdi he had no wish to compose anything but his elusive *Nerone,* and no greater desire than this:

> To have you set to music a libretto that I have written solely for the joy of seeing you take up your pen once more *per causa mia,* for the glory of being your collaborator, for the ambition of hearing my name coupled with yours, and ours

with Shakespeare's, and because this theme and my libretto
have been transferred to you by right of conquest. Only you
can compose *Otello*. The entire world of opera you have
given us affirms this truth. If I have been able to perceive
the Shakespearean tragedy's enormous capability of being
set to music (which I did not feel at first), and if in fact I have
been able to prove this with my libretto, it is because I placed
myself within the sphere of Verdian art. It is so because, in
writing those verses, I felt what you would feel when illus-
trating them with that other language—a thousand times
more intimate and mighty—sound. And if I have done this
it is because I wanted to take the opportunity in the prime
of my life, at an age when faith no longer wavers, to take
the opportunity to show you, better than by praises thrown
in your direction, how much I love and am moved by the
art that you have given us. . . . For Heaven's sake do not
abandon *Otello*; do not abandon it. It is predestined for you.
(O 158–59)

Then, in a shrewd stroke, to whet Verdi's appetite for the
work, he sent off a new text for what he and Verdi had already
discussed—an "evil Credo" for Jago (O 161). Verdi showed he was
back on board when he wrote: "This Credo is most beautiful, most
powerful, and Shakespearean in every way" (O 163).

Work on the librettos of *Otello* and *Falstaff* was a true collaboration. Verdi made structural suggestions as well as textual
corrections to the librettos, and Boito prompted Verdi to new
musical thoughts, especially in the handling of *Falstaff*'s source,
The Merry Wives of Windsor. They developed a fondly bantering
way of trading ideas, far from the exasperated and hectoring tone
Verdi used when dealing with the limits of earlier, less competent

librettists. Since Verdi wanted to keep his projects secret, they used a code, calling *Otello* "the Chocolate" (Il Cioccolato) and *Falstaff* "Megabelly" (Pancione). Though Verdi had to be edged ever so gently into work on *Otello*, he responded with glee to the idea of working again with Boito on another Shakespeare play. He had not written a comic work since the failure of his second opera, *Un Giorno di Regno*, forty years earlier. Boito had told him: "There is only one way to end better than with *Otello*, and that is to end victoriously with *Falstaff*" (F 7). Verdi felt the same. Asking for a sound argument for working at his age, he wrote Boito: "If you could find a single reason, and if I knew how to throw ten years off my shoulders, then—What joy! Being able to tell the public: *We are still here!! Make way for us!!*" (F 6). Boito not only wrote the librettos for the two operas, but engaged energetically in the casting and production details of each, working both with Verdi and with his friend Faccio in the preparation of *Otello* at La Scala.

The two men's jocular tone over Il Cioccolato became an almost giddy way of referring to Pancione in their letters. Boito wrote:

> I live with the immense Sir John, with Pancione, with the breaker of beds, with the smasher of chairs, with the mule driver, with the bottle of sweet wine, with the lively glutton, between the barrels of Xeres and the merriment of that warm kitchen at the Garter Inn. (F 16)

If Verdi's composing efforts slowed, it was said that Pancione was loafing or sleeping or drunk (F 121, 139). Or he was pining away for lack of sustenance: "Poor fellow! Since that illness which lasted four months he is scrawny, scrawny! Let's hope to find some good capon to reinflate his belly. . . . It all depends on the doctor! . . . Who knows? Who knows?" (F 131). If the tempo of work picked up, Falstaff was on a tear:

> Pancione is on the road that leads to madness. There are days when he doesn't move, sleeps, and is in a bad mood. At other times he shouts, runs, jumps, rages like the devil. . . . I let him sober up a bit, but if he persists, I'll have to put a muzzle and a straitjacket on him. (F 143–44)

Boito was so heartened by this good news of progress that he wrote back ebulliently:

> Evviva! Let him have his way, let him run, he will break all the windows and every piece of furniture in your rooms; never mind, you will buy others. He will smash the piano, never mind. You'll buy another one; let everything be turned upside down! But the big scene will be done! Evviva!
> Go! Go! Go!
> What pandemonium! But pandemonium as bright as the sun and dizzying as a madhouse!
> I know already what you will do. Evviva! (F 144)

In each of their two operas, the Verdi-Boito team faced a point that stumped and stalled them—the *concertato* end of Act 3 in *Otello* and the whole of Act 3 in *Falstaff*. They circled the problems, worrying them, chipping at them with new and overlapping suggestions, until they were solved, triumphantly. Boito late in his life remembered the two decades of his close and continuous work with Verdi as the high point of his life. The time also contained his years of romantic ardor for Eleonora Duse (1887–92).[4] There was enough of the Scapiglatura of his youth for Boito to have a *nostalgie de la boue* toward Duse's shoddy theatrical past. She had acted from childhood in provincial melodramas that he thought unworthy of her. He kept his affair with her secret while he tried to elevate her tastes and coach her in the classics, hoping she would equal her older French rival, Sarah Bernhardt. Despite Duse's later famous affair with Gabriele D'Annunzio, she considered her involvement with Boito the most elevating and spiritually rewarding interlude in her life.[5]

Boito translated *Antony and Cleopatra* for Duse, but did not attend the rehearsals or the premiere of his play, at a time when he was involved in every detail of the rehearsing and premieres of the Verdi operas. He did not want to bring the stage waif Duse, twenty years his junior, into the aristocratic milieu of Clarina Maffei, or into Verdi's exalted circle. He resisted a lasting commitment to her and to the idea of raising her daughter from an unhappy early marriage. Indeed, he never married anyone, though, against Verdi's initial doubts, he insisted that *Falstaff* had to end with a double marriage scene: "There have to be nuptials; without the weddings there is no contentment (don't mention this to Signora Giuseppina; she would start again to talk to me about matrimony!) and Fenton and Nannetta must marry" (F 11).

Boito and Verdi were brought closer than ever by the tragic end of their shared friend Franco Faccio, which interrupted for a time their work on *Falstaff*. Tertiary syphilis was destroying Faccio's mind. He would not repeat his conducting feat for *Otello* when *Falstaff* was completed. In 1889, when he was no longer able to manage La Scala's affairs, Boito and Verdi arranged for him to be employed as director of the Parma Conservatory (F 14). When

Faccio could not meet even his minimal tasks in Parma, Boito
filled in for him so that Faccio could continue to be paid his salary
(F 62–63). Boito had sent his friend to the Krafft-Ebbing center
for syphilis treatment in Graz (F 55), but the doctors said there
was nothing they could do for him. Verdi commiserated with
Boito: "The refusal in Graz, I think, is grave! It's a condemnation!
Poor friend Faccio! So good and so honest!" (F 60). Boito wrote to
Duse: "My sick friend has returned in worse shape. There is no
more hope. It is frightful to see him. I am spending my days, all
my hours, at his side" (F 61). Boito was at Faccio's bedside when
he died in 1891. The famous conductor was only fifty-one. Verdi
wrote to console Boito. The old fighters of the Scapigliati days
had now become as close as brothers:

> Poor Faccio was your schoolmate, companion, and friend in
> the stormy and happy times of your youth. And he loved you
> so much. In the great misfortune that struck him you rushed
> to him, giving him solemn admirable proofs of your active
> friendship. . . . Poor unfortunate Faccio! (F 146)

Boito and Verdi rallied from their shared sorrow to finish and
produce *Falstaff* in 1893. Boito was loath to let their partnership
end at that point. Though Verdi was now in his eighties, Boito
kept suggesting new projects to him. He said he could adapt his
translation of *Antony and Cleopatra,* done for Duse, into a libretto
for Verdi to set as an opera. He even tried to revive Verdi's long
interest in composing a *King Lear.* But this time Verdi's wife was
no longer conspiring with him for new projects. She wrote:
"Verdi is too old, too tired."[6]

The most Boito could do for new work from Verdi was to

mount his *Four Sacred Pieces,* already written, in a premiere. Boito had played a leading role in getting his *Otello* and *Falstaff* translated into French and performed in Paris. In 1898 he brought the *Sacred Pieces* before the public at the Opéra. Though Verdi, as usual, paid close attention to the proper casting and performance of the work, he did not feel well enough, at eighty-five, to go to the opening himself. He wrote to Boito:

> In going to Paris in my place you have rendered me a service for which I shall always be grateful. But if you reject any form of recognition I remain crushed by a burden I cannot and ought not to support. Well then, my dear Boito, let's talk frankly, without reticence, like the true friends we are. To show my gratitude I could offer you some trifle or other. But what use would it be? It would be embarrassing for me and useless to you. Permit me therefore, when you are back from Paris, to clasp your hand here. And for this handclasp you will not say a word, not even "Thank you." Further, absolute silence on the present letter. Amen. So be it. Affectionately, G. Verdi[7]

In the later years of Verdi's life, Boito visited him often, at his home, or in Genoa, or in Milan. He usually spent Christmas and Easter with him and Giuseppina—and after the latter's death in 1897, he was even more constant in attendance on her husband. When Verdi died, in 1901, Boito wrote to his French friend Camille Bellaigue:

> I threw myself into my work, as if into the sea, to save myself, to enter into another element, to reach I know not

what shore or to be engulfed with my burden in exertions
(pity me, my dear friend) too great for my limited prowess.[8]

Boito lived until 1918, and never finished his *Nerone*. He felt
the real distinction of his life lay in his collaboration with Verdi:
"The voluntary servitude I consecrated to that just, most noble,
and truly great man is the act of my life that gives me most
satisfaction."[9]

There have been other great collaborations between librettists and composers for the opera world—Da Ponte with Mozart,
Hofmannsthal with Strauss, Auden with Stravinsky. But none
worked more closely together, with deeper understanding of
each other's needs and merits, than Boito and Verdi. Verdi constantly urged Boito not to neglect his own opera *Nerone* (whose
libretto he had read and admired), while working on their joint
ventures. Boito understood music, and Verdi understood drama,
and each spurred the other to achieve greater things than they
had ever done alone. Theirs was an empathy that erased the
differences in their age (three decades apart). Despite his own
superior education, Boito never underestimated the lightning
intelligence of Verdi. Typical of their many discussions is Verdi's request to know how the English accent words like Falstaff or Windsor or Norfolk. Boito responded that the English
accent the first syllable in two-syllable proper names, though
he admitted that meter made him accent the last syllable of
Norfolk in Falstaff's little song "Quand'ero paggio" (F 121–23).
Thousands of little considerations like this went into their
years of weighing each word and each note in these colossal
scores.[10]

Frank Walker, the modern critic who made the English-speaking world appreciate the importance of Boito, paid him this tribute:

It was fortunate for us, and for Verdi, that among the younger generation there was this companion, so subtly intelligent, so unselfishly devoted. The more one learns of Boito the more he appears one of the noblest and purest spirits of the whole romantic movement.[11]

Verdi knew what Boito had done for him. After the successful premiere of *Otello*, and then again after that of *Falstaff*, he led Boito out with him to take the multiple curtain calls they had earned together.

Notes

1. Frank Walker, *The Man Verdi* (Alfred A. Knopf, 1962), pp. 451–52.
2. Ibid., p. 479.
3. Ibid., pp. 456–60.
4. Helen Sheehy, *Eleonora Duse* (Alfred A. Knopf, 2003), pp. 81–114.
5. Giovanni Pontiero, *Duse on Tour* (Manchester University Press, 1982), pp. 12–13.
6. Walker, op. cit., p. 502.
7. Ibid., p. 507.
8. Ibid. p. 509.
9. Ibid., p. 510.
10. In a less intense collaboration, Auden said that he worried that Stravinsky had never set an English text when they worked on *The Rake's Progress*. But when the composer mistook the accent on "sedan chair" (stressing the first syllable of "sedan"), he quickly corrected himself when the error was pointed out. W. H. Auden, *Forewords and Afterwords* (Random House, 1973), p. 433.
11. Walker, op. cit., p. 494.

7

Othello's and Otello's First Performers

{ Shakespeare's Actors

RICHARD BURBAGE, ROBERT ARMIN

Othello is a long play (3,685 lines), and its two lead roles are among the longest in the Shakespeare canon. Othello speaks 811 lines. Iago speaks even more lines than Othello (1,032). Iago needs so many lines because he is everywhere in and behind the action, messing with everybody's mind, and then turning aside to tell the audience what he is up to. The fact that Iago speaks more lines than the eponymous hero has led some to ask if the troupe's star, Richard Burbage, took this part. The puzzlement over which is the lead role has led, in performance history, to the alternation, night by night, between star players. In 1816, William Charles Macready and Charles Mayne Young traded the roles. In 1839, Macready and Samuels Phelps did so. In 1881, Henry Irving and Edwin Booth alternated; in 1950, Richard Burton and John Neville did it.

To see why this question has had such a long life, we should recognize that Iago might seem a natural role for Burbage. Iago has many long soliloquies, and frequent asides. These are the marks of certain Burbage roles, like Hamlet and Richard III. Shakespeare gives a character many soliloquies when that person is mounting a constant campaign of pretense. Hamlet is playing a madman. Richard is playing a pious leader. Iago is playing a warm friend to all he meets. Shakespeare expects Burbage to be so convincing in such assumed roles that he must stop at times and reveal to the audience what he is really doing.

Richard III is persuasive enough that he can win the heart of a woman whose husband he has just killed. Olivier in his film lets Richard convey a sense of decadent evil even at this moment, and Anne responds to the risky and kinky in the man. John Barrymore, on the contrary, used all his wooing charm as an ardent lover—and won by being quite different from what the soliloquies reveal of him. At the end of the scene, Barrymore asked, in a quizzical and wondering way, eyes down to the footlights, "Was ever woman in this humor woo'd?" as if amazed at his own versatility. Then he lifted his head and boomed out over the audience, "Was ever woman in this humor WON!" (1.2.27–28).

Hamlet plays the crazy man, though few modern performers let him do that. They want to maintain the nobility or dignity (or melancholy) of the man. But that underrates the tour de force effects Burbage was capable of. Hamlet does not wear motley, indeed; but his clothes, Ophelia tells us, are crazily disarranged. When Hamlet uses whirling words with Polonius, he comes across in modern performances as more teasing than crazed—which means that Polonius needs no shrewdness to suspect that "Though this be madness, yet there is method in't" (2.2.205–6). It was a mark of stage madness at the time that the afflicted person sang snatches of old songs, as Ophelia does. Burbage was a famously good singer.[1] He should sing things like:

For if the sun breed maggots in a dead dog, being a good kissing carrion (2.2.181–82)

To a nunn'ry, go (3.1.139)

To a nunn'ry, go (3.1.149)

For O, for O, the hobby-horse is forgot. (3.2.135)

Why, let the strooken deer go weep,
  The hart ungalled play,
For some must watch while some must sleep,
  Thus runs the world away. (3.2.271–74)

"For thou dost know, O Damon dear,
  This realm dismantled was
Of Jove himself, and now reigns here
  A very, very"—pajock. (3.2.281–84)

For if the King like not the comedy
Why then belike he likes it not, perdy. (3.2.293–94)

The King is a thing— . . .
Of nothing (4.2.28–30)

Hide, fox, and all after. (4.2.31)

Let Hercules himself do what he may,
The cat will mew, and dog will have his day. (5.1.291–92)

He should probably also chant "inconsequent" repetitions like "Words, words, words" (2.2.192) or "except my life, except my life, except my life" (2.2.216–17).

Hamlet's denunciation of womankind in the scene with

Ophelia—"You jig and amble, and you lisp" (3.1.144)—is often taken as solely reflecting his personal anguish; but that, too, was part of the fool's "mad" repertory—as in Feste's exchanges with Olivia or Thersites' with Cressida. Leslie Hotson rightly said that Hamlet's railing in that Ophelia scene vents "the old tradition of histrionic ribaldry" from a fool.[2] Shakespeare's philosophical fool, Robert Armin, asked in his book, "Where's the devil?" and answered: "In usurer's bags, in women's paint."[3] Ophelia is shocked not by the ribaldry but by Hamlet's obvious craziness:

> O, what a noble mind is here o'erthrown!
> The courtier's, soldier's, scholar's, eye, tongue, sword,
> Th' expectation and rose of the fair state,
> The glass of fashion and the mould of form,
> Th' observ'd of all observers, quite, quite down! (3.1.150–54)

Hamlet stays true to his "antic disposition" when he calls himself "O God, your only jig-maker" (3.2.125), playing on the fact that the fool leads the jig at a play's end.

It is clear that Iago should never let anyone in the play know what he is really up to. That is why he has to reveal himself in eleven soliloquies or asides, totaling 144 lines in all, three-quarters the length of Emilia's entire role.[4] It is often asked how Othello could succumb so entirely to Iago's reports of Desdemona's infidelity. But all characters in the play believe whatever Iago tells them—not only all the men he deals with but Desdemona too, and his own wife, Emilia. When Desdemona says that she will work to restore Cassio to Othello's favor, Emilia says:

Good madam, do. I warrant it grieves my husband
As if the cause were his. (3.3.3–4)

That is: even his wife thinks that Iago, who engineered Cassio's dismissal, is actually grieving for it. If he so completely fools the woman he has lived with, then no one seems exempt from the nets he weaves. His manipulation of others is so powerful because no one has ever been let in on the secret of his malicious scheming. That is why he must keep revealing *to us* the evil that is hidden from everyone else. His frequent soliloquies and asides allow him to savor in isolation the evil he exults in.

So the role would allow Burbage to repeat the virtuoso effects of his other soliloquy-laden parts, Hamlet and Richard. It would even allow him to sing "'And let the canakin clink'" (2.3.69). On the other hand, Othello bears the full tragic weight of the play, and only Burbage had the stature to give such suffering its proper effect. We shall see that Verdi's Otello has a cosmic grandeur. Only Burbage played such roles—Coriolanus, for instance, or Mark Antony.

Who then played Iago? It is often noticed that Iago has a sharp satirical humor. "I am nothing if not critical" (2.1.119). Covered with darkness under Brabantio's window he gives his fleering gifts their rein:

you'll have your daughter cover'd with a Barbary horse, you'll have your nephews neigh to you; you'll have coursers for cousins, and gennets for germans. (1.1.111–13)

One of Iago's ingratiating poses is that of a lovable clown. He pretends to Othello that he is too naive to dissemble. Harley Granville-Barker described Iago's "chameleonlike ability to adapt

himself to changes of company and circumstance, his sympatheti-
cally parasitic faculty of being all things to all men."⁵ Gary Schmidgall makes the brilliant suggestion that it was the quick-witted
jester of the company, Robert Armin, who played Iago.⁶ What
Viola says of fools in *Twelfth Night* would apply very well to Iago:

> This fellow is wise enough to play the fool,
> And to do that well craves a kind of wit.
> He must observe their mood on whom he jests,
> The quality of persons, and the time;
> And like the haggard, check at every feather
> That comes before his eye. This is a practice
> As full of labor as a wise man's art (3.1.60–66)

There is a declared clown in the play *Othello*, but he has only
two short scenes (3.1.3–29, 3.4.3–22), which Honigmann calls
"probably the feeblest clown scenes in his [Shakespeare's] mature
work."⁷ They are crude scenes, not the subtle and intellectual
sort Shakespeare invented for Armin, and they are usually omitted in modern performance.

Armin was an intellectual himself, a theorist of folly who
published a book on the subject and wrote his own plays. Many
have supposed that any clown or jester role written after Armin
joined the company must have been performed by him. But
Shakespeare had more than one way to use this talented man. It
used to be thought, I noted earlier, that Armin played the Fool in
King Lear. But Shakespeare took care to delay the Fool's entrance
until Cordelia had been offstage for some time, and he carefully
reported the Fool's death before Cordelia returned at the play's
end. Clearly the same boy actor played the innocent Fool and the
gentle Cordelia. Armin was better used as Edgar, feigning mad-

ness and speaking as the fool "Poor Tom." Edgar even plays the dramatist as he creates Gloucester's "fall" over the cliff at Dover.

Leslie Hotson rightly notes that Burbage takes the fool's role away from Armin in *Hamlet,* and he suggests that Armin, the expert on folly, may have helped Burbage learn how to play that fool's part. Armin was probably the First Gravedigger in the play, but Hotson thinks he would also have doubled Polonius, doing the pompous fool as a variant of his witty fool's role.[8] Armin, in his own and others' plays, was adept at doubling parts, or even, by changes of voice, carrying on dialogues and fights with himself in two different personae. In Ben Jonson's *Every Man Out of His Humor,* playing Carlo, he acted out a dispute between two courtiers. In Armin's own play, *The History of the Two Maids of More-clacke,* Armin played both the natural fool, Blue John, and the artificial fool, Tutch.[9] In his book, *Quips Upon Questions,* he pretended to be a member of the audience heckling him during his act.[10] Armin's gift for mimicry allows him, as Feste in *Twelfth Night,* to pose as Sir Topas when deceiving Malvolio.

David Wiles argues, from a concatenation of references to Armin in his various roles, that he was small and almost dwarfish— he is the only adult actor known to have played with a children's troupe.[11] The lack of menacing size would accord with Iago's nonintimidating appearance to everyone in the play, where he is treated almost as a mascot. Iago, like Thersites (another Armin role), resents the commanding appearance of the hero. In dramatic lineage, Iago is derived from the Vice of the old morality plays— the witty devil who provided so much energy in Tudor theaters.[12] The Vice was also the ancestor of Richard III, so funny and wicked, and of Falstaff, the jocular tempter tutoring Prince Hal in criminal pursuits. Iago fits neatly into this company of intelligent deviants.

⸱ *Verdi's Singers*

FRANCESCO TAMAGNO, VICTOR MAUREL

When Verdi completed *Aida,* at age fifty-seven, he thought he had closed out his career in opera. But his publisher, Giulio Ricordi, and the aspiring librettist Arrigo Boito schemed with Verdi's wife, Giuseppina, to draw him back into active composition. They knew his reverence for Shakespeare, and they spent years playing on that. Beginning in 1879, when Verdi was sixty-six, they tried to interest him in Shakespeare's *Othello* as an opera. They insisted that Rossini's *Otello* had done a disservice to the great English dramatist (O 14). Verdi at first resisted what he treated as a plot against his peace, but he was intrigued—indeed fascinated—by the subject of Shakespeare's play, and especially by Jago (as he spelled it).[13]

As a way of playing with the idea of the opera, while not finally committing himself to it, Verdi plied an artist friend, Domenico Morelli, with requests that he paint "Jago." Morelli responded with a plan to make Jago look sinister, with "the stamp of a Jesuit" (O 117). But Verdi wanted a "scoundrel with the face of a righteous man" (O 18). "A figure such as this can deceive anybody—even his wife, up to a point. A small, malicious figure arouses suspicions in everyone and deceives no one" (O 118). Verdi understood that Shakespeare's Iago needs a universal believability.

Verdi's conception of the character would be stated by Boito in the *Otello Production Book* composed under Verdi's supervision:

> The greatest error, the most vulgar error an artist attempting to interpret his character could commit, would be to represent him as a kind of human demon, to put a Mephistophelian

sneer on his face, and to give him Satanic eyes. Such an artist would show that he had neither understood Shakespeare nor the opera we are here discussing. . . . He must be handsome and appear jovial and open and almost good-natured. . . . If he were not so attractive in his personal charm and his apparent honesty, he would not be able to become as powerful as he does through his deception. (O 485–86)

As Verdi toyed, coyly, with the idea of composing the opera, he kept referring to it as *Jago*. But in time he realized that Jago is a provoker, not a protagonist. He wrote to Boito, six years into their discussion of the work:

Jago. He is (it's true) the demon who sets everything in motion; but Otello is the one who acts. *He loves, is jealous, kills, and kills himself.* For my part, it would seem hypocritical not to call it *Otello*. I prefer it if they say, "He tried to fight a giant and was crushed," rather than, "He tried to hide behind the title of Jago." If you are of my opinion, let's start baptizing it *Otello*, then. (O 200)

Boito, in the production book, endorsed this view of Otello as the greater figure: "Otello goes through the most horrible tortures of the human heart—doubt, rage, lethal depression" (O 483).

Even after Verdi began composing the work, he retained a diffident pose, saying that he might not allow it to be performed: "Shall I finish it? Maybe yes. Shall I give it? It is difficult for me to answer this" (O 211). Another way Verdi found for putting off a full commitment to the project was to doubt that the opera could be properly cast, rehearsed, and performed. He knew from the outset what vocal types he needed for the two main roles—a warlike tenor for Otello, an insinuating baritone for Jago. He did not labor under the liability that Rossini experienced in his *Otello*, with its tenor Otello, tenor Iago, tenor Doge, tenor Rodrigo, and tenor gondolier. To overcome Verdi's casting doubts, Ricordi and Boito sent him endless reports on possible singers, almost all of whom Verdi judged inadequate. The exception was the man Verdi early identified as his preferred Jago, the French singer Victor Maurel (1848–1923), who had sung Amonasro in the Paris *Aida* that Verdi conducted in 1880.

Even this relationship was rocky at the outset. Maurel, a cultured man—a writer and a painter—had sung the title role in Verdi's revision of his own *Simon Boccanegra* (1881), but he was temperamental, with his own ideas of how a role should be played, and Verdi warned Giulio Ricordi, while preparing *Simon*, that Maurel could be "crazy" (O 37). Then, to make matters worse, Maurel caught wind of a possible new opera from Verdi, and he campaigned to be the first Jago (O 188). Verdi, who hated being pressured, put him off. Still, the composer admired the artistry of this intelligent singer. He began to compose the role of Jago with Maurel in mind. Like many a foreigner, Maurel pronounced his Italian with special care, and this was what Verdi liked best about him. "Nobody enunciates as clearly as he does, and in the part of Jago there are so many parlandos that need to be said quickly and sotto voce, which no one could do better than he" (O 208). When Verdi began to coach Maurel for the role, he inserted new material to exploit his gifts (O 276). Here is his advice on performing the role:

> In this part, one must neither *sing* nor (with few exceptions) *raise one's voice*. If I were a singing actor, for example, I would speak it all in a whisper, *mezza voce*. (O 262)

This was the same advice Verdi had given Varesi for singing Macbetto. Though Maurel was known to substitute his own views for those of composers and directors, reviews show that he followed Verdi's instructions carefully, at least in early performances of *Otello*. The *Times* of London wrote, for instance,

> As an actor he realized the character of the plausible villain with a distinctness seldom witnessed even in the spoken drama. He was honest Iago all over, soft-spoken, and looking most innocent when he aimed the most poisonous shafts at the defenseless breast of the Moor. (O 703)

Jago's evil "Credo" in Act 2, delivered with a defiantly full voice, registered with great impact from its contrast with the softer, more insinuating delivery of other lines.

Casting the other male lead was a different matter. Francesco Tamagno (1850–1905), who would later seem born for the part of Otello, was initially considered the wrong man for it by Verdi. Tamagno had sung in Verdi's revised *Simon Boccanegra* (1881) and *Don Carlo* (1884), in which Verdi thought the singer had been loud and powerful, but without art or nuance. Like Maurel, Tamagno campaigned for the part—almost fatally. When Giulio Ricordi, sounding the tenor out, gave the impression that he had the role guaranteed him, Verdi responded harshly:

> No matter what you may say, the engagement of Tamagno was a mistake which can jeopardize everything. I have told you, and I repeat, that I don't believe he can succeed either in the duet that ends the first act, or in the last scene; thus two acts would end coldly. It is not possible. (O 207)

Some think that Otello is a kind of Italian Heldentenor role—all it takes is clarion power. Verdi never thought that. In fact, he feared it, and almost disqualified Tamagno for fitting too well that description:

> After he has ascertained that Desdemona has been killed [though] innocent, Otello is breathless; he is weary, physically and morally exhausted; he cannot and must not sing any more, except with a half-muffled, veiled voice, but with a reliable one. This is a quality that Tamagno does not have. He must always sing with full voice, without it his sound becomes ugly, uncertain, off-pitch. This is a very serious matter and gives me much to think about. I prefer not to give the opera if this point of the score is not brought out. (O 201)

Ricordi argued that Verdi's coaching, for which he was by then famous, would mend Tamagno's ways. Verdi was not sure he could work such a miracle, and shuddered to think of the time and energy it would take (O 256). But in fact he did bring about some artistry in the man who became the most famous Otello of all time. But Bernard Shaw, a shrewd evaluator of voices, agreed with Verdi's first view of Tamagno's limitations. After hearing him in London, Shaw wrote:

> [As Otello] there was an Italian, Tamagno, undoubtedly a quite exceptional artist, whose voice seems to have reached the upper part of the theater with overwhelming power, though to others some of the current descriptions of its volume seemed hyperbolical. His voice, at any rate, had not the pure noble tone, nor the sweetly sensuous, nor even

the ordinary thick manly quality, of the robust tenor; it was nasal, shrill, vehement, sometimes fierce, sometimes plaintive, always peculiar and original. Imitation of Tamagno has ruined many a tenor, and will probably ruin many more, but the desire to produce such an effect as he did with *Addio, sante memorie* is intelligible to anyone who rightly understands the range of an Italian tenor's ambition. (O 733)

Even Tamagno's partner in all the early runs of the opera, his Jago, Victor Maurel, had misgivings about Tamagno's trumpet blasts. He later wrote:

The ideal of vocal power necessary for Otello was provided with astonishing intensity by the creator of the role, Francesco Tamagno. But we think it dangerous to instill in the minds of Italian interpreters of Otello the idea that this kind of extraordinary vocal power is a condition sine qua non of a great interpretation.

In support of this point, we shall cite an example which will be confirmed by everyone who, like ourselves, has heard the singer about whom we are going to speak. We must recall the memory of the tenor [Mario] Tiberini.[14] No one, in our estimation, knew how to realize as he did such powerful effects in tragic roles with the quite ordinary means with which nature had endowed him.

We are therefore convinced that if a Tiberini were to sing Otello today, he would, by the intense stressing of the accent of the musical phrase, completely compensate for his lack of natural power, and would electrify an entire hall in the most violent passages of the role.

Those tenors, then, who have the ambition to sing Otello should not be intimidated by the true accounts of the unique voice of the creator of the role. Instead, they should keep in mind this important observation: after ten minutes, an audience becomes accustomed to the sonorous timbre, no matter how great it may be. What captivates and always enthralls an audience is the dramatic energy and variety of vocal dynamics. (O 532)

The success of lyrical tenors singing Otello—like Giovanni Martinelli, or Francesco Merli, or Giacomo Lauri-Volpi—bears out Maurel's view of the matter. Nonetheless, the public loved Tamagno's sheer volume. His opening blast in the role ("Esultate!") became his trademark, and audiences would follow him to his hotel and shout to his balcony until he came out and launched that victory cry. Tamagno's voice was hailed as a force of nature. The famous conductor Tullio Serafin, who played violin in performances of *Otello,* had heard Tamagno earlier, as he rehearsed the title role in Rossini's *William Tell:*

> Tamagno's voice was not so huge as many people think, but rich in vibrations that expanded like a ringing trumpet. I'll never forget a rehearsal of *Tell* at La Scala when I was playing viola in the orchestra. Tamagno had sung sotto voce until the third act. To try out his full voice, he let loose a high C in his aria; sympathetic vibrations reflected off the harp, which was next to me, and struck me in the ear with such force that I thought I had received a slap. It was some time before I began to hear again normally.[15]

Verdi did train Tamagno to some subtlety, but the more polished Maurel made fun of his partner's crudities, and Tamagno complained of this to Verdi (O 318). Verdi tried to reconcile the singers, with only partial success. In fact, the feud between them may have sharpened Maurel's onstage drive for Otello's undoing. Over the years Tamagno kept working on the guidance Verdi had given him. Further refinements were added to the role when Tamagno sang it under Toscanini in the 1899 revival (which ran for nineteen performances). Toscanini, who was playing cello in the orchestra for the premiere of the opera, had Verdi's own view about subtler aspects of the title role, as one can tell from his handling of Ramón Vinay in the 1948 recording of the work.

The singer in *Otello* with whom Verdi was least satisfied took the role of Desdemona. There was great pressure for him to accept Romilda Pantaleoni (1847–1917), who had succeeded as Margherita in Boito's own revised opera *Mefistofele* (1876). She was the lover of the opera's first conductor, Boito's and Verdi's friend Franco Faccio, who worked closely with Verdi in preparing the singers and orchestra. She was a forceful performer, and that, in Verdi's eyes, was the problem. "Such a passionate, fiery, violent artist, how will she be able to control and contain herself in the calm, aristocratic passion of Desdemona?" (O 220). After she came to Verdi's home at Sant'Agata and sang for him, Verdi wrote to Faccio:

> Signora Pantaleoni's voice becomes cutting at passionate points, and in high notes a little too biting; she gives too much metal, so to speak. If she could get used to singing with a little more head-voice, the *smorzato* [softening] would come easier to her and her voice would also be more secure and natural. (O 134)

Though he let Pantaleoni take the part, he was not satisfied with her performance:

La Pantaleoni, in spite of her dramatic instinct for high-strung parts, could not feel and understand Desdemona. To judge *terre à terre,* the character of Desdemona, who allows herself to be mistreated, slapped, even strangled, who forgives and commends herself [to God], seems a bit stupid. But Desdemona is not a woman, she is a type. She is the type of goodness, of resignation, of sacrifice. Such beings are born for others, unconscious of their *own self.* Beings that partly exist and that Shakespeare has put into poetic form and has deified by creating Desdemona, Cordelia, Juliet, etc.—these are types that perhaps can only be compared to the Antigone of the ancient theater. (O 300–301)

Verdi worked patiently with Pantaleoni, changing the "Willow Song" to suit her voice (O 245–46) and transposing the Act 2 quartet a halftone lower to accommodate her. Even so, he later regretted yielding to Faccio's pleas for her (O 101–2). He reluctantly let her keep the role in Brescia, but he wrote Ricordi: "You speak of her singing off-pitch? She has always sung off-pitch" (O 393). He kept trying other sopranos as Tamagno and Maurel took the opera around the world, but none of them quite worked, and Shaw took apart the poor woman who played the role in London.

But in general, Verdi's thorough, almost fanatically detailed preparations—for the libretto, the score, the rehearsals, the orchestra, and the singers—raised the professional level of Italian opera, and prepared the way for the scintillating later triumph of

Falstaff. Bernard Shaw, a devout Wagnerian who often mocked Italian opera, was stunned by La Scala's production of *Otello* when it reached England:

> The grip of the drama on the audience, the identification of the artists with their parts, the precision of execution, the perfect balance of the forces in action, produced an effect which, for the first time, justified the claims of Italian opera to rank as a form of serious drama united to purposeful music. The usual romantic explanations of this success were freely offered—Italian aptitude, great artists, La Scala, Wagnerian methods, and so on—but thorough preparation was the real secret. (O 732)

He especially praised the conductor and orchestra: "The artistic homogeneity of performance, the wonderful balance of orchestra, chorus, and principals, stamp Faccio as a masterly conductor" (O 732).

Tullio Serafin believed that "Verdi had a lot to do with the revolution in operatic acting; he spent hours coaching singers onstage, even in his advanced age."[16] By the time of *Otello,* Verdi had achieved a complete authority over every part of a production—costumes, sets, lighting, and every musical aspect of the work. As Verdi himself put it:

> No one, *absolutely no one,* at the rehearsals, as usual—I have complete authority to suspend the rehearsals and prevent the performance, even after the dress rehearsal, if either the execution or the mise-en-scène or *anything else* in the way the theater is run should not be to my liking. (O 241)

Notes

1. Burbage was commissioned, along with the boy star of the troupe, John Rice, to sing in the 1610 festival for the Prince of Wales.

2. Leslie Hotson, *Shakespeare's Motley* (Rupert Hart-David, 1952), p. 24.

3. Charles S. Felver, *Robert Armin, Shakespeare's Fool* (Kent State University, 1961), p. 26.

4. Richard III speaks 145 lines in soliloquy, and Hamlet tops all others with 217 lines.

5. Harley Granville-Barker, *Otello* (Heinemann, 1885), pp. 144–45.

6. Gary Schmidgall, *Shakespeare and Opera* (Oxford University Press, 1990), p. 209.

7. E. A. J. Honigmann, *Othello* (Arden Shakespeare, 1997), p. 65.

8. Hotson, op. cit., pp. 95, 104.

9. See David Wiles, *Shakespeare's Clown* (Cambridge University Press, 1987), pp. 138–58.

10. Felver, op. cit., pp. 28–29.

11. Wiles, op. cit., pp. 148–50, 158–59.

12. Ibid., pp. 1–10.

13. Jago and Diego are Spanish forms of Jacobus (English James). The apostle James was supposed to have been martyred in Spain, where he is honored as San Diego (or Santiago) de Compostella. Shakespeare scanned Iago as three syllables, with the accent on the middle one. Verdi and his librettist treated Jago as disyllabic.

14. Mario Tiberini (1826–1880) sang the complex coloratura part of Rossini's Otello as well as Verdi's Alvaro in *La Forza del Destino* and Riccardo in *Un Ballo in Maschera*.

15. Tullio Serafin interview, *Opera News*, April 29, 1961, p. 1.

16. Ibid.

8

Cosmic Reach

Perhaps the first word that should come to mind in connection with the dramatic character of Othello is not "black" or "jealous" but "grandiloquent." He "speaks big." His imagination has the seven-league boots of Marlowe's Tamburlaine:

> Like to the Pontic Sea,
> Whose icy current and compulsive course
> Nev'r feels retiring ebb, but keeps due on
> To the Propontic and the Hellespont,
> Even so my bloody thoughts, with violent pace,
> Shall nev'r look back, nev'r ebb to humble love,
> Till that a capable and wide revenge
> Swallow them up. Now, by yond marble heaven,
> In the due reverence of a sacred vow
> I here engage my words. (3.3.453–62)

His life opens backward into vast traveled spaces:

> I spoke of most disastrous chances?
> Of moving accidents by flood and field,
> Of hair-breadth scapes i' th' imminent deadly breach,
> Of being taken by the insolent foe
> And sold to slavery, of my redemption thence

And portance in my travel's history;
Wherein of antres vast and deserts idle,
Rough quarries, rocks, and hills whose heads touch heaven,
It was my hint to speak—such was my process—
And of the Cannibals that each other eat,
The Anthropophagi, and men whose heads
Do grow beneath their shoulders. (1.3.134–45)

Such "tall tales" may not seem likely to impress sober Venetian senators sitting in emergency council, yet they strike such awe into the counselors that they dismiss the charges of Brabantio against Othello. The Duke himself says, "I think this tale would win my daughter too" (1.3.171).

But twentieth-century critics judged Othello's story more harshly than did the senators he addressed. Grandiose rhetoric was suspect in their eyes. T. S. Eliot found Othello's attitude proud and pagan, like that of Seneca, not humble and Christian, like that of Dante. F. R. Leavis found in Othello's words a "self-idealization" by which "self-pride becomes stupidity." G. Wilson Knight took them as "false bombast." Anthony Hecht found the rhetoric "colored by a self-regard and self-consciousness" that undermine nobility.[1]

But high-flown rhetoric was expected in "larger-than-life" characters of the Renaissance. It is the natural mode of men like Shakespeare's Titus Andronicus, Julius Caesar, Coriolanus, Mark Antony, or Achilles (in *Troilus and Cressida*). Would the critics find all of them self-idealizers to the point of stupidity? These characters talk the language of Chapman's Homeric heroes. Their "heads hit the stars," and there is something cosmic in their careers, their loves, their hates, their destined ends. Alastair Fowler calls such Renaissance heroes "stellified"—people moving in a shower of meteoric brilliance.[2] That is how Othello talks:

> Excellent wretch! Perdition catch my soul
> But I do love thee! and when I love thee not,
> Chaos is come again. (3.3.90–92)

> Methinks it should be now a huge eclipse
> Of sun and moon, and that th' affrighted globe
> Did yawn at alteration. (5.2.99–101)

> Here is my journey's end, here is my butt
> And very sea-mark of my utmost sail.
> . . . .
> O ill-starr'd wench,
> Pale as thy smock! when we shall meet at compt,
> This look of thine will hurl my soul from heaven,
> And fiends will snatch at it. Cold, cold, my girl?
> Even like thy chastity. O cursed, cursed slave!
> Whip me, ye devils,
> From the possession of this heavenly sight!
> Blow me about in winds! roast me in sulphur!
> Wash me in steep-down gulfs of liquid fire! (5.2.267–68, 272–80)

Othello's majesty is established in the first act of Shakespeare's play, which Arrigo Boito felt he had to cut from his libretto for Verdi's opera—all 686 lines of plot set in Venice. This upset the balance of the play, since the opening act presents Othello as calm, commanding, rational, respected, and wielding great authority—in short, the perfect foil to the impassioned and out-of-control figure in the later acts. Othello, as an outsider in the ancient Venetian state, is seen as actually more civilized than his political hosts. He is above each situation wherein he is placed. The tone is perfectly struck when Brabantio brings a night watch to arrest Othello. The Moor calmly says, "Keep up your bright swords," with the emphasis on "bright" because of the smiling follow-up—"for the dew will rust them" (1.2.59). Boito kept the first part of the line, but without its original context. In the opera, Otello angrily interrupts a nighttime duel with a stentorian "DOWN THE SWORDS" (*ABBASSO LE SPADE*).

Another sign of Othello's authority is the way he deals with the trial for witchcraft he is subjected to. As I noted in discussing *Macbeth,* witchcraft was a deadly issue in Shakespeare's England, where far more people were put to death for it than were killed in Salem, Massachusetts. There is some reference to witchcraft in every one of Shakespeare's plays. But witches are treated by Shakespeare as low and disreputable. Macbeth's ambition makes him credulous of the witches, while Banquo stands apart and views them skeptically.

In *Othello,* it is the "civilized" Venetians who take seriously the witch accusations, while Othello magisterially dismisses them with a smile. The danger Othello stands in is hard for a modern audience to appreciate. The Duke tells Brabantio that the man he has charged with witchcraft will be punished to the full extent of harsh laws against this crime:

> Who e'er he be that in this foul proceeding
> Hath thus beguil'd your daughter of herself,
> And you of her, the bloody book of law

You shall yourself read in the bitter letter
After your own sense; yea, though our proper son
Stood in your action. (1.3.65–70)

Shakespeare piles up the charges of witchcraft to mount a great challenge for Othello to face down by the sheer power of his presence, his rhetoric, and his reasoning. "Practice" and "abuse" were technical terms of witchcraft—as when Hamlet says that the devil "perhaps, / Out of my weakness and my melancholy . . . / *Abuses* me to damn me" (2.2.600–603). So Brabantio, trying to explain his daughter's aberrant action, asks:

Is there not charms
By which the property of youth and maidhood
May be *abused*? (1.1.171–73)

And Brabantio arrests Othello with this indictment:

Damn'd as thou art, thou hast enchanted her,
For I'll refer me to all things of sense,
If she in chains of magic were not bound
. . . .
Judge me the world, if 'tis not gross in sense,
That thou hast *practic'd* on her with foul charms,
Abus'd her delicate youth with drugs or minerals
That weakens motion. I'll have't disputed on,
'Tis probable, and palpable to thinking.
I therefore apprehend and do attach thee
For an *abuser* of the world, a *practicer*
Of arts inhibited and out of warrant. (1.2.63–65, 72–79)

Brabantio appeals to the Duke for judgment:

> She is *abus'd*, stol'n from me, and corrupted
> By spells and medicines bought of mountebanks;
> For nature so prepost'rously to err
> (Being not deficient, blind, or lame of sense)
> Sans witchcraft could not. (1.3.60–64)

> It is a judgment main'd, and most imperfect,
> That will confess perfection so could err
> Against all rules of nature, and must be driven
> To find out *practices* of cunning hell
> Why this should be. I therefore vouch again
> That with some mixtures pow'rful o'er the blood,
> Or with some dram (conjur'd to this effect)
> He wrought upon her. (1.3.99–106)

The Senate questions Othello:

> Did you by indirect and forced courses
> Subdue and poison this young maid's affections? (1.3.111–12)

Othello, in his great council speech, had mocked the charges against him:

> I will a round unvarnish'd tale deliver
> Of my whole course of love—what drugs, what charms,
> What conjuration, and what mighty magic
> (For such proceeding I am charg'd withal)
> I won his daughter. (1.3.90–94)

After he gives the heroic account of his life that won Desdemona, he sums up:

> She lov'd me for the dangers I had pass'd,
> And I lov'd her that she did pity them.
> This only is the witchcraft I have us'd. (1.3.167–69)

Even before the arrival of Desdemona (the only defense witness Othello has called), the Duke acquits the defendant:

> I think this tale would win my daughter too.
> Good Brabantio,
> Take up this mangled matter at the best. (1.3.171–73)

Othello admits in his speech that he is an outsider in Venice—indeed, it is the exotic nature of his adventures that attracts Desdemona. It might even be suspected that he repeats (or invents) superstitious tales, as of

> The Anthropophagi, and men whose heads
> Do grow beneath their shoulders. (1.3.144–45)

But the oddest details in the speech are taken from respected reports of European explorers. The men whose heads do grow beneath their shoulders are taken from Sebastian Münster's *Cosmographie* (1572).[3] Othello views the foreign world, in which he was a captive of the Turks, through Venetian eyes. He has risen to be admiral of the Venetian fleet by many years of fighting for the republic. We later learn that his brother fought beside him and was killed in the city's wars (3.4.137). We get later confirmation of what we would expect of a Venetian official, that he is a Christian, who holds his baptism dear (2.3.343). When he puts down the brawl in Cyprus, he speaks for his adopted civilization:

> Are we turn'd Turks, and to ourselves do that
> Which heaven hath forbid the Ottomites?
> *For Christian shame,* put by this barbarous brawl. (2.3.170–72)

Though some famous actors had worn Muslim or Arab dress as Othello, Verdi rightly insisted that he should be costumed as a Venetian. In Cyprus, Othello *is* Venice. His is the majesty of the law. His language, and his bearing, have a cosmic reach.

This gives the lie to A. C. Bradley's famous claim in his influential book, *Shakespearean Tragedy*, that Othello, a tale of domestic strife, lacks the universal implications of *Hamlet* or *King Lear:*

> In *King Lear,* the conflict assumes proportions so vast that the imagination seems, as in *Paradise Lost,* to travel spaces wider than the earth. In reading *Othello,* the mind is not thus distended. There is a comparative confinement of the imaginative atmosphere.[4]

In *Othello,* the breakup of the marriage of Othello and Desdemona is not simply a domestic misfortune. It undermines the authority of Venice. It brings disorder to Cyprus. It allows the triumph of a cosmic vision of evil voiced by Iago. It brings back the suspicion of witchcraft in Othello. It is this cosmic scale that Boito and Verdi will find in the work.

⟨ *Verdi*

Since Boito and Verdi eliminated the first act of Shakespeare's play, they did not have means for establishing Otello's calm mastery before the council, or the ironic way he deflects the charges of witchcraft. Verdi more than makes up for this in the heroic nature of Otello's music. By a preemptive strike at anything that might make Otello look petty, Verdi opens with an apocalyptic storm, as if the whole universe were cracking open. Otello, by riding out this storm, is instantly heroic. The screaming sense of doom resembles the "Dies Irae" of Verdi's *Requiem*.

An organ rumbles throughout (three notes a semitone apart sounding simultaneously), piccolos dash out lightning streaks, horns howl like the wind, trumpets stutter, gongs strike, and bass drums thunder. Harmonic slides make it seem as if the very frame of the universe were dissolving. Verdi gives us a paradoxically precise articulation of disintegration. The chorus sings in mounting panic:

> Lampi!
> Tuoni!
> Gorghi!
> [Lightnings!
> Thunders!
> Maelstroms!]
>
> Treman l'onde! Treman l'aure!
> Treman basi e culmini!
> [Seas shake! Skies shake!
> Depths and heights shake!]

Great choral expressions of terror wash over each other like sheets of driving rain. The organ's continued roar gives an ominous undertow. The *Otello Production Book* from the premiere says,

> The organ should have its pedal stops ready, as indicated in the score, as well as stops. On the first note of the orchestra, the organ should open these stops and maintain the sound without interruption until the end of the storm. (O 491)

Verdi at first thought the organ should cease when Otello, arriving, utters his victory cry, but then thought better of it. Otello should emerge from the storm, full of its energy even as he beats it back. He is an elemental force himself.

Three of the traditional four physical elements—air, earth, and water—are jumbled about. Phrases of terrified prayer ("Lord, this blaze of storm . . .") are punctuated with screaming downward plunges of the orchestra which give the odd effect of horses' frightened neighings, as if the four horsemen of the apocalypse were somehow riding the wild winds. "The whole earth is convulsed" (*Spasima l'universo*).

This whole spasm of music is the background for what has been called the most dramatic entry in all of opera. Otello's opening cry goes up to high G-sharp on the word "Pride," then pulls the Turks down a whole chromatic octave slide to end in a sour G-natural for the "sea" in which the Turks are sunk:

Esul*tate*: L'orGOGlio musulmano
sepolto è in mar!
[Take heart! The PRIDE of the Muslims
is now buried in the sea.]

Tamagno recorded this trademark opening in 1903, when he was fifty-three. He still had all his bright high bellowing, but he was getting short of breath. Instead of one downward drive on the phrase *"L'orgoglio musulmano sepolto è in mar,"* he stops for air after *"musulmano."* He does the same in the next sentence, breaking what should be a mounting phrase, *"ciel è GLORIA,"* with a breath just before the climactic *"GLORIA."*

Otello should not be a matter of mere volume. That improbable Otello, Beniamino Gigli, shows what phrasing, dynamics, coloration can do to convey control and command. In his recording of the "Esultate," the comparatively pinched syllables *"e-sul"* blossom out in the broad vowel of *"-TAT-e,"* and he drives down the Turks in one magnificent sweep. I played the record to an opera lover who told me he never before realized how the *acciaccatura* on *"l'uragano"* sealed Otello's whole opening statement. (Tamagno sang it with a double mordent, the curlicue ornament his generation favored, one that seems more frilly than the nail-it-down *acciaccatura*.) Alan Blyth, not normally a Gigli fan, writes that his "Esultate" is "rich and amazingly powerful from a basically lyric voice."[5] Verdi and Maurel were right when they said there was more in Otello's music than Tamagno's sheer force.

Verdi deserves all the credit for this coup de théâtre. Shakespeare has Othello arrive in Cyprus after 180 lines of the second act. His arrival follows two others—that of Cassio in his ship, then that of Iago and Desdemona. Othello's first words are to Desdemona, who has just arrived herself: "O my fair warrior!" (2.1.182). He instantly goes on to say that he will never know greater joy than his reunion with her. She shows her independence by saying that this cannot be their best moment, since her love will increase (2.1.193–95).

Boito wanted to save their expression of love for the great duet closing Act 1, so Desdemona is not on the battlement when Otello lands there. Boito has Otello ask Jago where she is, and he responds that she awaits him in the castle. Only then does Otello, in Boito's first draft, address the crowd: "Honest Jago, good Montano, and all you here, take joy and sound the festival." The Cypriots greet this with their acclaim: "The pride of the Muslims is plunged into the sea" (O 217). This is too fumbling for Verdi. He wants to take that boast of the crowd and give it to Otello at the very outset. He wrote Boito:

> You know that the storm (musically speaking) continues during Otello's entrance and until after the Chorus of the six-syllable verses. There are too many lines in Otello's solo, and the storm gets too broken up. It seems to me that the scene would not lose a thing if it were shortened by four lines, and then I would make a phrase for Tamagno, perhaps an effective one. In fact, it is already made: "Take heart! The pride of the Muslims . . ." (O 217)

From the words Boito gave Otello, Verdi takes just one, *"Esultate"* (Take heart). The rest are transferred from the Cypriots, and the great entrance is achieved.

After Otello leaves the scene, his impact is still felt in the victory dance of the Chorus. Boito has it deliriously reenact the defeat of the storm in a scatter of short lines:

> Dispersi, distrutti,
> Sepolti nell'orrido
> Tumulto piombâr.

[Broken up, ruined down,
Interred in a dreadful
Sea-swell's plunge.]

If the opening storm gives a picture of cosmic convulsion, the love duet later in the act gives us a sense of cosmic harmony, of a deeper order in the universe. Stendhal had pointed out the greatest flaw in Rossini's *Otello,* the lack of love music for Otello and Desdemona. Without a deep love, Otello's jealousy is mere vanity.[6] Rossini did not even give the principals a duet until the final death scene. Boito, who knew Stendhal's book, took care to remedy this flaw with a grand-scale love duet in the very first act, for which Verdi composed the greatest love music of his entire career. Otello disappears after his trumpeting entrance, while Jago manipulates Cassio around the victory celebration, getting him drunk to provoke the riot that brings Otello back to the stage. The thunderous "DOWN the swords" shows him commanding human tumult as he did the storm of his entrance. This makes the serene love duet all the more impressive by contrast. The opening is mesmerizing. "But now dense night extinguishes all tumult." Muted cellos make soothing gestures. (One of the cellists at the premiere in Milan was Arturo Toscanini.)

This is unlike most love duets. In them, one lover addresses the other in fervent song, the loved one responds by repeating the ardent song, and then they blend in joint profession of their love. Here Otello and Desdemona spin out their fondness in separate reveries—not talking past each other, as Macbetto and Lady do in their great first-act duet, but as if finishing each other's sentences, like a married couple that do not need to say what each feels, so intimately do they intuit what the other is thinking. Boito's poetry is at its best here. Otello relaxes into this eloquent sigh: "My thrashing heart is gathered by this enfolding and held safely in." The enfolding (*amplesso*) referred to is not, yet, Desdemona's embrace, but the vast starry hold of night upon him. Then muffled memories of war are recollected in tranquillity: "Sound out war and world-rendings, if after such vast hate comes this VAST LOVE."

Here as throughout the opera, Desdemona takes the initiative, pouring out her love at every turn. Boito cleverly gives her the words that Othello used to describe his wooing in Shakespeare's first act. From her they are more sweetly persuasive, and they begin with a ravishing three words: *"Te ne rammenti?"* which Verdi marked *"come una voce lontana"* (as in a voice sounding far off); Spike Hughes describes the spell that is cast by Desdemona's words:

This is a breathtaking moment, created by such a superb example of simple scoring that it should be contemplated in silent and humble meditation by composers of all ages every night before they go to bed. Verdi uses two flutes and a piccolo to play the triad C-E-G, a harp with a rising *allargando morendo* arpeggio across four octaves, two bassoons that double the low C and G of the four solo violoncellos' two bottom open strings, and first and second violins and violas, each divided into two parts. One of the greatest lessons to be learned from the way this chord is scored is what is left out. There is nothing, except the climbing harp arpeggio, between the low G of the violoncellos and bassoons, and the G two octaves higher of the violas. Perhaps the open, but silent, C and G strings of the violas and the G strings of the violins vibrate in sympathy; perhaps it is the ear's imagination; but it is a chord that sounds much fuller and richer than one is led to expect from what is written down.[7]

The bliss that Desdemona brings to the duet continues, calming Otello. When he remembers his own wars (to the marking *"ppp, come un mormoria,"* very softly, as a rumble), most tenors get too blaringly martial here, which made Verdi think Tamagno could not handle the love duet. Desdemona takes him back to his quieter boyhood ("You told me of the glowing desert, the burning sands, of your maternal earth"), and he senses the cosmic harmony of her singing: "A brightness descends upon my darkness, a paradise and stars that bless." Otello now launches his own melody, "You loved me for my perils passed," and she repeats the tune, "I loved you . . ." "You loved me . . ." "I loved you. . . ." Otello is raised to the point of ecstasy as the orchestra melts in a kind of orgasmic bliss: "Joy engulfs me so entirely that I swoon with panting." After the kiss that will end their lives in Act 4, the lovers commune again with the stars. He sings, "The fiery Pleiades have plunged into the sea." She answers, "Night lingers." Then, with sparkling harp music to suggest the humming night, he sings, "The love star is glowing." Almost all tenors belt this out, but Verdi marked the first three syllables *pp*—*"Ve-ne-re"*—then the music blazes up briefly at *"SPLEND"*—with a long diminuendo *"de-e-e"* that Desdemona softly joins, singing his name. The Heldentenor tradition of most performing Otellos is certainly not true to the subtle love music Verdi composed—or to the mystical calm he wanted in this vision of cosmic harmony.

Notes

1. T. S. Eliot, "Shakespeare and the Stoicism of Seneca," in *Selected Essays* (Harcourt, Brace & Company, 1932), pp. 110–11; F. R. Leavis, *The Common Pursuit* (Chatto & Windus, 1952), pp. 146–47; G. Wilson Knight, "The Othello Music," in *The Wheel of Fire* (Oxford University Press, 1930), p. 102; Anthony Hecht, "Othello," in *Obbligati: Essays in Criticism* (Atheneum, 1986), p. 72.

2. Alastair Fowler, *Time's Purpled Masques: Stars and Afterlife in Renaissance English Literature* (Oxford University Press, 1996). See also Frances Yates, *Astraea: The Imperial Theme in the Sixteenth Century* (Ark, 1975), pp. 29–87.

3. See E. A. J. Honigmann, *Othello* (Arden Shakespeare, 1997), pp. 5–6.

4. A. C. Bradley, *Shakespearean Tragedy* (Macmillan, 1908), pp. 176, 181.

5. Alan Blyth, *Opera on Record* (Hutchinson, 1979), p. 319. Gigli did not have the vocal heft to sing the whole role in the house, but his two excerpts in the otherwise awful 1941 movie *Mamma* are impressive indeed.

6. Stendhal, *Life of Rossini*, translated by Richard N. Coe (Orion Press, 1970), pp. 210–11.

7. Spike Hughes, *Famous Verdi Operas* (Chilton Book Company, 1968), p. 441.

9
Cosmic Ruin

Boito and Verdi began their work on the opera fascinated by Jago. Verdi kept begging his artist friend Domenico Morelli to paint the soul of Jago (assuming he had a soul). Boito wrote, in his introduction to the *Otello Production Book*, "Jago is the real author of the drama. He creates the threads, he gathers them up, he arranges them, he intertwines them" (O 485). Yet some claim that the men's greatest departure from Shakespeare is their Jago. These critics think they turned him into a simple stage villain, a pure devil modeled on the Mefistofele in Boito's own opera of that title. Their principal evidence is the Act 2 monologue "Credo in un Dio crudel," which they liken to "Son lo spirito che nega" in *Mefistofele*. Yet Verdi called the "Credo," when Boito delivered its final version to him, "Shakespearean in every way" (O 163). Was he mistaken?

We should begin with a structural problem presented to Boito by Shakespeare's text. It was argued earlier that frequent soliloquies and asides are necessary to Iago as Shakespeare conceived him. The man must always seem sincere to those on the stage—gruff and soldierly in general, with special appeals to different characters. He is sympathetic to Othello, innocently flirtatious with Desdemona, supportive of Roderigo's love-quest, grieving with Cassio, above a vile use of the handkerchief in Emilia's eyes. He is so patently benign that the first word that springs to people's lips when they mention him is "honest." It is almost a Homeric epithet for him.

Shakespeare wants him to be so convincing in his various masks that the play must be stopped, at frequent intervals, to remind us that he is actually up to no good.

But it is hard to insert frequent soliloquies into the musical flow of an opera. There must be a musical preparation for the episode, thematic and harmonic, then it must be played out in the slower rhythms of sung as opposed to spoken delivery, and it must be fitted with musical connections to the texture of what follows. Boito gave Jago asides that play against the ongoing music ("Oh, mio trionfo"), and he let him exult alone over the fallen Otello (but counterpointed against the triumphal trumpets that keep the general action going). Boito decided to replace the many soliloquies of Shakespeare with one grand overall statement of Jago's evil mind.

This is the "Shakespearean" element Verdi found in the "Credo."

It cannot be denied that there is considerable distance between Shakespeare's Iago and Boito's Jago. The former is descended from the medieval Vice of the morality plays, the latter from the swaggering diabolism of the Romantic Era.

But Jago is even further from Boito's Mefistofele than from Shakespeare's Iago.

Boito's devil appears, in the prologue to the opera, in the context of the heavenly court with its angelic choirs. He is the Satan of the book of Job, challenging God and defying him. Jago, by contrast, *represents* God; he is vile only because God is vile. Mefistofele rebels against God. Jago carries on God's own evil campaign in an evil world made by this evil God. It is a nihilist vision. Admittedly, Boito in *Mefistofele* was setting the poem of the Romantic Era poet Goethe, but that is Goethe's adaptation of the medieval legend of Faust, and the general setting is still orthodox in its medieval theology. That is the last thing that could be said of Jago.

The "Credo" is a savage satire on the ecclesiastical Creed as set by endless musicians, as in the great Masses of Bach and Beethoven. The orthodox Creed asserts the articles of faith in repeated (anaphoric) form: "I believe in God the Father. . . . And [I believe] in his only-begotten Son. . . . And [I believe] in the Holy Spirit." Jago too lays out the articles of his faith in repeated "I believes":

I believe in an evil God.
I believe that the evil I intend I perform according to Fate.
I believe that the holy man is a buffoon.
And I believe that man is the toy of malevolent chance.

Jago explicitly compares his belief with the church's in the words "I believe with as true a heart as the widow in church believes." He screws home the unshakeableness of his faith by raising each iteration of "Credo" a half tone, and making each a variation on the five-note opening assertion of faith, those pounding chords of a firm faith, like the pillars of his structured confidence. Beethoven opened his "Credo" with just such chords of affirmation.

Budden finds Lisztian touches of devil-dance in this false-churchy Creed, with its shakes, trills, drums, cymbals, and triangles. After the phrase "from the seed of the cradle" Budden hears "an orchestral guffaw of semiquavers" (B 3.358). This, and the fact that a tradition has grown up of ending the monologue with a fiendish laugh, has led some to dismiss the "Credo" as a standard picture of the melodramatic villain. But the *Otello*

Production Book, issued by Giulio Ricordi and approved by Verdi on the basis of the first performance, gives a very different view of the ending. "At his final words, *È vecchia fola il Ciel,* he should shrug his shoulders then, turning, walk upstage" (O 529).

This direction points the way to a very different interpretation of the last part of the monologue. After the words "from the seed in the cradle" and the orchestral guffaw, Jago's voice sinks into the quiet minor-key phrase "to the worm in the grave." Then the opening assertion of faith is repeated in a softened and pianissimo form before Jago says, "After so much mockery comes—Death." (Pause.) "And then?" (A longer pause.) In a sinking voice, "Death is Non-Being." The orchestra flares up—*it* does the laughing mock: "Heaven's an outworn fable." But if Jago does not laugh—if he just shrugs his shoulders—it is a *self*-lacerating conclusion. It is true that Toscanini let Giuseppe Valdengo issue the laugh in his recording. But there is no mention of the laugh in the score, and Verdi—who said Violetta should not cough to signal her consumption, and Riccardo should not laugh as he sings "È scherzo od è follia"—liked to let the music speak the message.

It is wrong, therefore, to give Jago a cheaply triumphant laugh, like a poised Mefistofele. It is superficial to think of Jago as torturing only those around him. He tortures himself. He is angry—he bases his creed on anger: "I name him [the cruel God] in my wrath" (*che nell'ira io nomo*). How then are we to read those quiet hesitations on *"E poi? E poi?"* Are they just devilish teasings of the audience? It seems, rather, an expression of wistful regret, of genuine anguish at the meaninglessness of everything. The flare-up of the orchestra carries him almost involuntarily back to the harsh articles of his creed. Here is the real point of the "Credo." *Aida* indicts religion. *Don Carlos* indicts the state. In

Otello, Jago indicts the universe. He lashes out in a nihilistic frenzy. He means to match Otello's cosmic reach with his own cosmic ruin. He wants to destroy Otello as a symbol of society and what it prizes. Tamburlaine is a self-destroyer in his greatness. Jago is a destroyer of greatness in Otello. His anger is, at a deeper level, the anger of Cassius at Caesar's greatness in Shakespeare's *Julius Caesar*:

> Why, man, he doth bestride the narrow world
> Like a Colossus, and we petty men
> Walk under his huge legs, and peep about
> To find ourselves dishonorable graves. (1.2.135–38)

Jago expresses a voracious lust for destruction, an attitude Chesterton voiced through the nihilist warrior Ogier in his *Ballad of the White Horse*:

> There lives one moment for a man
> When the door at his shoulder shakes,
> When the taut rope parts under the pull,
> And the barest branch is beautiful
> One moment, while it breaks.[1]

This is one way in which the "Credo" does resemble *Mefistofele*. Boito's own opera opens in a cosmic way, with an apocalyptic and visionary prologue. The "Credo" also has a cosmic sweep, in the text and in the music, so thunderous and inclusive. Jago says that his own evil comes from the very origins of the world, that vileness was in the first seed or atom of being—"*Dalla viltà d'un germe o d'un atòmo.*" Jago arises from "the primordial mud" (*fango originario*). All men are Fate's toys from "the seed in the cradle to the worm in the grave" (*Dal germe della culla / Al verme dell'avel*). That Boito and Verdi knew they had created a sensational blasphemy came out in 1889, when Verdi was composing an Ave Maria as a harmonic exercise. He told Boito this was his fourth Ave, after Dante's version and those in *I Lombardi* and *Otello*. Boito responded: "Plenty of *Ave Marias* will be needed for the Holy See to forgive you Jago's *Credo*." And Verdi shot back: "You're the main culprit who needs to be granted a pardon for Jago's *Credo*" (B 3.421).

In the opera's opening scene, after Otello's entrance and exit, and the brief victory dance, there is a fire chorus. Three of the universal elements—earth, sea, and air—were in the storm music. But except for the lightning flashes the fourth element was largely absent. That is made up in the fire ritual that appropriately follows on Jago's mutterings with Roderigo. Boito makes this an oddly equivocal celebration. Fire is a dangerous thing to indulge. It warms, but it also sears. It lures the moth. There is something ominous in saying that bride and spouse burn together as the palm and sycamore are burning in this bonfire. Fire passes as swiftly as love. It dies. Boito's brilliant lines bristle with a merry menace. He writes four quatrains, each with an *abab* rhyme scheme:

Fuoco di gioia! l'ilare vampa
Fuga la notte col suo splendor.
Guizza, sfavilla, crepita, avvampa,
Fulgido incendio che invade il cor.

Dal raggio attratti vaghi sembianti
Movono intorno mutando stuol,
e son fanciulle dai lieti canti,
e son farfalle dall'igneo vol.

Cosmic Ruin

Arde la palma col sicomoro
Canta la sposa col suo fedel;
Sull'aurea fiamma, sul lieto coro
Soffia l'ardente spiro del ciel;

Fuoco di gioia rapido brilla!
Rapido passa, fuoco d'amor!
Splende, s'oscura, palpita, oscilla
L'ultimo guizzo lampeggia e muor.

[Flame for rejoicing, merry blaze-up!
It banishes the shining night.
It wriggles, throws sparks, crackles, grows,
Bright conflagration enters the heart.

Drawn to its rays, dim shapes
circle it, a shifting crowd.
some maidens with their happy songs,
some moths now made to fly in flame.

The palm burns with the sycamore,
As bride sings with her faithful spouse.
And on the golden love, the happy song,
Breathes the burning heaven-soul.

Flame for rejoicing, quickly it flares!
Quickly, too, passes the flame of love.
It is shining, shadowy, panting, wobbling.
Its last wriggle blazes, then dies.]

Just before this deceptive song, Jago was manipulating
Roderigo. Just after it, he manipulates Cassio, getting him drunk.

No wonder we must read Boito's poem ironically, as if we can see through the flames Jago's evil smile.

After the fire ceremony strikes its equivocal note, Jago sings his equivocal drinking song. It seems hearty and companionable, but we know it is a trap set to get Cassio drunk. Though it is in 6/8 time, it has the swaggering tread of a march tune—a very masculine *brindisi,* as opposed to the drinking songs of Violetta or Macbetto's Lady. Jago punctuates it with a sinisterly sliding *"Be-e-va. Be-e-va!"*—a kind of musical leer as he sees his plan working, a signal that he is laughing at his audience, not with it. He climaxes it with a chromatic slide down a whole scale on the word *"Beva,"* then two leaps up, *"Be-VA, Be-VA!"*

This is not a static song, like most *brindisi.* A great deal is going on in and around it. Cassio sings phrases of a countermelody at the end of each stanza, and Jago "whispers" to Roderigo at the success of their plan. Then, at the end of the second stanza, the music itself seems to be getting drunk, as new instruments do a bridge of bubbly syncopation. At the end of the third stanza, the orchestra's march tread has become a lurching accompaniment as the drunken Cassio is unable to get out his own phrases (sung in jumbled bits, in a choked voice, says Verdi—*"voce soffocata"*). The drinking song was just a pretext for provoking Cassio into a brawl. All of the ensembles in this opera advance the narrative in complex ways.

Jago's diabolical side comes out in asides and comments meant to be understood by the audience but not by the characters onstage. In an aside just before the "Credo," he says to Cassio's departing back:

Vanne.
Vanne. La tua meta già vedo.

Ti spinge il tuo dimone,
E il tuo dimon son io.
[Be off!
Be off where I see you going—
where your devil drives you—
and your devil? That's me.]

Jago is at his most insidious when he is pretending to dis-
suade Otello from doubting Desdemona or urging him not to
be jealous. In an eerily serpentine phrase later in Act 2, he warns
Otello: "Fear jealousy, lord. It is a dark hydra, gaunt, blind—it
poisons itself with its own venom, tearing its own breast." While
warning against poison, he is injecting it. Budden describes the
passage (B 3.361): "A spine-chilling transition marks the first mention of jealousy, whispered into Otello's ear. The strangeness of
the [harmonic] progression is underlined by the use of the full
orchestra *pianissimo*"—as of a powerful force held back in.

An even more insidious exchange occurs when Jago pretends
that Otello has compelled him to describe Cassio's dream while he
was sleeping with him. It begins in a rocking way (*pp*), almost like
a lullaby—in fact, the most chilling thing about this monologue
is its mesmerizing beauty. Verdi wants it all to be pianissimo and
sotto voce. As Jago tells his false story, he takes on the whispery
voice of the supposedly sleeping Cassio, and shows that he is having a wet dream. At the words "A heavenly ecstasy drowns me,"
the chromatic slide is orgasmic. Joseph Kerman captures the effect:

With so robust a composer as Verdi, perhaps the most vivid
marker of this [his dramatic development] is the way he now
learned to cultivate understatement—in, say, Jago's narrative

of Cassio's dream in Act II. Starting like a diatonic barcarolle ("honest Iago") touched by a single sleepy chromaticism, this piece turns into a pornographic nightmare as the chromatics seep deeper and deeper into an evil parody of aria form. Balancing phrases begin their orderly modulations, only to drop disconcertingly back to the tonic; the opening music returns ambivalently in the orchestra, accompanying Jago's devious mumbling. The orchestra sums up the growing chromaticism in a pianissimo sequence of dizzying sensuousness.[2]

The orchestra tiptoes away from the dream, in a series of little rises, before Jago gives a "sunrise" awakening as if innocent of what he has done.

We have only one recording from this opera by the original Jago, and it is this dream. Victor Maurel made it in 1903, when he was fifty-five years old. He begins with a nice *mezza voce,* as marked, but he does not always keep to the *pp* markings, and (like Tamagno) he substituted "curlicue" mordents for the two marked *accacciature.* He does go from the preceding phrase straight without a breath into the orgasmic slides at *"estasi . . ."* When hoping to learn the composer's intent in creators' records, especially those made a decade and a half after a premiere, we should remember what John Gielgud wrote in his letters. After directing Richard Burton in his New York *Hamlet,* he came many weeks later to see a performance. All the bad habits he thought he had corrected had sneaked back in. Other directors have told me the same thing. Performers get bored or adventurous or forgetful. So our records from Tamagno and Maurel give us only an approximation of what they originally did for the demanding Verdi.

Cosmic Ruin

Even when Otello thinks he is taking charge of his fate, and Jago is just standing by, Verdi finds a shrewd way to reveal the real truth of the relationship between them. At the end of Act 2 Otello launches into his great oath, "Sì, pel ciel," to thumping chords of affirmation, as he swears by the eternal that he will be revenged on Cassio and Desdemona. Jago joins in only after Otello has laid out the oath, but when he does so it becomes obvious that Otello was singing the countermelody, not the basic one. Jago supplies that, showing he is in charge and Otello does not even know it. When, at the end, they sing in unison, *"Dio Vendicator"* (God the Revenger), Jago is aware that there is no crime to be revenged—he made it up. In the circumstances, his use of God's name here is strictly blasphemous.

Only at the end of Act 3, when Otello is unconscious, lying in a coma after his epileptic fit, does Jago openly show his relation with the Moor, planting his foot on the fallen man and saying, with a sarcastic shake, "Here is the Lion!" In the opening storm, Montano sights the admiral's ship and cries: "It's the winged lion!" That refers of course to the symbol of Venice at the prow of the ship, but it is also Otello's ship, and he is identified with it. When Jago grinds his foot into Otello, he is bringing down not only Otello, but Venice. While the offstage chorus is singing the praise of Otello and Venice, he is making a mockery of that. He wants, symbolically, to bring down the universe.

Notes

1. G. K. Chesterton, *The Ballad of the White Horse* (Marygrove College Press, 1993), p. 52.
2. Joseph Kerman, "The Verdi Blues," *New Republic*, January 10, 1964.

10

Between Cultures

The great mystery of *Othello* is how the commanding, even majestic, figure of Act 1 becomes the hysterical, even barbarous, figure of the late acts. The obvious but superficial answer is that Iago is a genius at whittling down greatness. But why was Othello, despite his many strengths, vulnerable to such manipulation? The poet Anthony Hecht, in a brilliant essay, depicts Othello as caught between cultures.[1] He is a Venetian and a Moor, a Christian and an ex-Muslim, brilliant at war and a novice at love. His life has been lived outside any stable community but the army-navy he used against the Turks on the outskirts of the Venetian empire. He is respected by his troops. Montano, the governor of Cyprus before his arrival, says of him:

> . . . 'tis a worthy governor.
> . . . .
> For I have serv'd him, and the man commands
> Like a full soldier. (2.1.30, 35–36)

He is respected in Venice, but he has to know that for every Duke there are many Brabantios there—a man who once loved him, had him often at his house, but reacts with rage at the thought of his daughter in his dusky embrace.

His life has been that of the camp, and one reason he trusts Iago is that he has shared that life with him, for longer times and in closer contact than with any nonmilitary Venetian, including his wife. Iago plays on that fact. How can Othello be sure that he understands Venice? Iago attacks Venice in general as a way of undermining Othello's trust in one Venetian in particular—Desdemona:

> I know our country disposition well:
> In Venice they do let God see the pranks
> They dare not show their husbands; their best conscience
> Is not to leave't undone, but keep't unknown. (3.3.201–4)

When Iago says "our country" here, he does not mean "the country you and I, Othello, share" but "the country I share with other Venetians." He is subtly excluding Othello from Venice. That puts him back in the no-man's-land of war, where Othello has seen Iago fight—why should he not trust a man so proved?

Exiled thus, what is he to make of Desdemona? Iago says she belongs back in Venice (which is not a compliment in his eyes):

> Not to affect many proposed matches
> Of her own clime, complexion, and degree,
> Whereto we see in all things nature tends—
> Foh, one may smell in such, a will most rank,
> Foul disproportions, thoughts unnatural. (3.3.229–33)

Othello does not have her "clime, *complexion,* and degree." He finds it hard to go against such an expert on Venice as Iago. . . . He is out of place, and cannot judge the place involved.

Good as he is at war, command, and leadership, Othello is a beginner in certain things. Both Hecht and Auden note that he seems inexperienced in sex, stressing his own chastity as well as (originally) Desdemona's. He asks the council to grant Desdemona's wish to go with him to Cyprus:

> Vouch with me, heaven, I therefore beg it not
> To please the palate of my appetite,
> Nor to comply with heat (the young affects
> In me defunct) and proper satisfaction;
> But to be free and bounteous to her mind. (1.3.261–65)

Hecht says of Othello: "He has interested himself in no one before Desdemona, and his interest in her is of an uncommon purity."[2] Auden says that Othello and Desdemona are so inexperienced that they idealize the other, a dangerous thing when they finally encounter reality. "Here, the moment you doubt, you're sunk." He concludes that "Othello and Desdemona should not have married."[3]

Verdi

The Desdemona of Boito and Verdi is very different from Shakespeare's, though Verdi said he was taking her from Shakespeare's "types" of pure womanhood. So Boito does not include the sexual jesting with Iago. She instantly wins the hearts of the Cypriots, who devote one of their local festivals to her.

It is like the flower ceremonies to the Virgin Mary. That gives a further touch of blasphemy to Jago's determination to besmirch her purity. As society disintegrates around her, she alone retains the soaring lyricism of the love duet from Act 1, with its cosmic harmony. She is the test by which others fail—Jago by reviling her, Cassio by endangering her with his suit, Emilia by her trust in her husband, and Otello by his suspicion of her.

The treatment she gets from these people could not be further from the union of those who celebrate her. Cypriot children, sailors, and women sing separate hymns of praise to her, prolonging the serenity of the love duet into Act 2. The children sing: "We offer you the lily, sweet star, which in the hand of angels was carried up to heaven." The sailors offer shells and pearls, singing: "We wish, Desdemona, with our gifts to adorn you like a sacred image. A golden bride the halo of dew surrounds, as it shimmers in the sun." She responds to this homage, picking up the melody of the first (group) song, with a quatrain (rhyme *abab*):

> Splende il cielo, danza
> l'aura, olezza il fior.
> Gioia, amor, speranza
> cantan nel mio cor.
> [Shines heaven, and the air
> Dances, to scent of the flower.
> Joy, love, and hoping fair
> Sing in me at this hour.]

Boito, who created a blasphemous parody on the Creed for Jago, creates a pious homage to Desdemona. Verdi gives to each group music of an appropriately different texture and rhythm, from the celestial to the childlike (mandolins and little harps), to a hornpipe suggestion for the sailors. As this sweet interlude ends, Desdemona's voice rises to a celestial high D.

From this moment things begin to disintegrate under her heavenly attempt to keep the world harmonious. When Otello grows wrathful at her pleading for Cassio, she tries to soothe his brow with her handkerchief. He grabs it and throws it on the ground, where Emilia picks it up. Then Desdemona launches what turns out to be the most action-filled quartet imaginable. She sings an overarching melody of love, a long caressing line— Budden says, "Not even Bellini achieved such a span" (B 3.365). But Otello is not paying attention to her. He is muttering to himself that perhaps she betrays him because he is black, or old. Jago is setting up his own muttered action, trying to wrest the handkerchief from Emilia, and she sings fragments of resistance. The story is going forward on many levels, as opposed to the static ensembles of the past. As Spike Hughes says, "The clear differentiation between the characters and the simultaneous presentation of three dramatic situations places it among Verdi's finest achievements in this form."

Desdemona tries again to hold together a fragmenting world. In Act 3, when Otello rages at her in fury for not producing the handkerchief, she lifts up another of her sweet long tunes of pleading: "I pray heaven for you with these tears of mine—the first tears you ever forced from me." It does no good, and later, when in the presence of the Venetian envoy Otello throws her to the ground, she soars into her last overarching melody, this time expressing not hope but hopelessness: "That calm and quickening sun, which gives joy to sky and sea, will not dry the bitter tears of my pain." This launches the last public scene of the opera, the finale of Act 3, over which Verdi and Boito had debated for a long time, to make it top the previous two finales and the quartet of Act 2.

The result is the longest and most complex concerted finale in Verdi's work, one that shows in effect the Venetian state disintegrating. After she pours out her lyrical lament, four unaccompanied

voices sing the disjointed reaction—shock (Emilia), emptiness (Cassio, musing that his new governor's office gives him
no joy), moroseness (Roderigo, on losing his "angel"), and fear
(Lodovico, looking at a raging Otello). Then an elaborate churning figure brings everyone onstage in a wailing lament for the
terrible situation, with the women's chorus supplying a weeping
cadence—all are engaged but Otello and Jago, who darkly perfect their murder plans. When at last Otello joins the company it
is at a climax, to shout his curse at Desdemona. The crowd with-
draws in horror, and Otello falls into his epileptic fit, allowing
Iago to put his foot on "the Lion."

If Desdemona through almost all the opera is the voice of
beauty trying to harmonize the society around her, Otello has
been withdrawing more and more into a tortured isolation.
In powerful soliloquies, he sings farewell to his glory in Act 2
("Ora e per sempre"), and of the crumbling of his faith in everything in Act 3 ("Dio mi potevi"). When Jago banters with Cassio about Bianca, Otello stands so far apart from them that he
thinks they are talking of Desdemona. In the Act 3 finale, he is
the only one who does not join in the great lament the others are
singing. This progressive extrusion from the human company is
the fulfillment of that cultural displacement that Anthony Hecht
described. The tamer of the storm, the quieter of brawls, is now
a lonely dweller in a psychological no-man's-land.

Verdi goes deeper and deeper into Otello's despair. Only the
sympathy he creates for this forlorn man allows us not to despise
him. The "Ora e per sempre" is martial, a farewell not only to his
military profession but to the feats for which Desdemona fell in
love with him, according to the Act 1 duet. It is self-promoting,
self-pitying, and self-destroying.

In "Dio mi potevi," Otello says he could have borne any suffering but one—a knowledge of Desdemona's betrayal. Take away his trust in her, and everything else turns to ashes. The aria begins with what Alan Blyth calls "the A flat test":

The whole of the vocal part in the first section is written on that note, except when it three times falls to E flat. Otello is deceptively resigned, calm; all the poignancy of his situation is expressed in the gradually rising, yearning phrases in the orchestra.[4]

How does Verdi get such a powerful effect from such simple means? Dyneley Hussey considers the matter:

There are all kinds of imponderables—of tonality and rhythm and part-writing—which combine to turn a monotone and a descending scale into the most tragic imaginable expression of disillusionment and of that inner emptiness of the human soul after it has given way to uncontrolled anger. There is first the tonality, the rare and remote key of A flat minor; when there are more than four flats in the signature, one may be certain that Verdi means tragic business. Then, there is the rhythm of the descending scale, which proceeds steadily enough, indeed, but has each note prefaced by a sharply accented triplet of semiquavers on the off beat. Add to this a syncopated accompaniment in the bass, and introduce the whole by a double-dotted descending chromatic scale from dominant to tonic, and you have this complex piece of simplicity.[5]

As the monologue turns into the major, there is a kind of sunrise as Otello mounts to a memory of the delirious joy he had in the sun of Desdemona's love. Then, in a savage turn, he bids Mercy herself veil her face in darkness as Desdemona confesses and dies.

The racing of mood after mood, each perfectly expressed in the music, shows the interior collapsing of Otello's mind. It is a tour de force, showing Verdi's ability to make drama of one man's interior state.

In the last act, we have a lonely and isolated Desdemona to match the Otello already stranded in his own emptiness. Otello, once in command of all around him, now has no connection with anything around him. Desdemona, the harmonizer of every company, has lost her own serenity. Like Rossini, Verdi takes from Shakespeare the "Willow Song," an expression of her loss, harking back to a time when her maid experienced the suffering that little Desdemona could not feel then but can only remember now.

She begins the song with composure, but a wind blows up, unsettling her (as the storm had frightened Desdemona in Rossini's "Willow Song"). The refrain, *"Salce, salce"* (Willow, willow), should be sung "in a far-off voice," an effect perfectly captured by Rosa Ponselle in her 1924 recording.

After she says good-bye to Emilia in a passionate last cry between them, she begins the Ave Maria. If, as Alan Blyth says, the tenor singing Otello has an A-flat test in the "Dio mi potevi," then Desdemona has an E-flat test as she begins this prayer (sotto voce, in Verdi's direction), since she sings the first half of the prayer repeating that note forty-four times. Then with a portamento she sweeps up to middle C to sing the petitions of the prayer, "Pray for us sinners. . . ." To hear Ponselle go from her velvet chest voice up, without a breath, to the sweet pleadings of the prayer's end is to find, at last, the Desdemona Verdi kept searching for and never found.

Otello enters Desdemona's bedchamber to a menacing duet played by double basses to a nervously jittery figure punctuated by *pp* single bass drum stops, which Boito compared to "shovels-ful of earth being dropped into a grave." Dyneley Hussey says: "The agitated staccato muttering that comes to a halt on a soft thud of the big drum is like some idea repeating itself over and over in the brain."[6]

After Otello kills Desdemona and is discovered, he gives his last great speech, "Niun mi tema," which Tamagno recorded. It is a stentorian delivery, slow, with heavy vibrato. He glances back at his past with *"O GLOOOOR-ia,"* then drops down to a quiet *"Otello fu"* (Otello's done). Some of the speech is sung unaccom-panied, as from a well of loneliness cut off from all sympathy—as when he addresses the murdered Desdemona: *"Tu, come sei pal-lida, e stanca, e muta, e bella"* (You, how pale you are, how weak, how silent, how lovely). Verdi coached Tamagno intensively to get just the right pathos into these lines, and he still has it. He sounds tortured on *"pia creatura nata sotto maligna stella"* (devoted being born beneath a baleful star). He is unaccompanied again when he cries out *"DESDEMONA! DESDEMONA! Ah, morta, morta,"* and when he cries, *"Ho un'arma ancor!"* (I am still armed!). He ends with a kiss on her dead face, to the surge of the kiss music in the love duet of Act 1, as if a memory of cosmic bliss were wafting up briefly from the cosmic ruin that Otello's world has become. He is cut off before singing the last syllable: *"Un altro ba-[cio]."* Tamagno *sings the last syllable,* then gasps with an asthmatic intake and outlet of breath, followed by an interpolated *"Ah!"* followed by a dying groan. None of this is written in the score, though most Otellos even when they do not sing the last syllable replace it with some kind of death rattle. They do the same thing when Verdi has Riccardo in *Ballo* die before he can finish his final phrase. Admittedly, the *Otello Production Book* says that Otello "utters the final syllable in a breathless sob" (O 673). But in the score the singer is not to utter the final syllable, and remember that Verdi condemned the idea of a death rattle in Lady's sleepwalking scene. He went on to say that Violetta should not cough and Riccardo should not laugh in "È scherzo od è follia." He wanted the music alone to do the weeping, laughing, and dying, with no extra sound effects from the singers. It is interesting to note that Gigli, often charged with tastelessness, just lapses into silence after "*ba*"—as it is written. "The rest is silence."

Notes

1. Anthony Hecht, "Othello," in *Obbligati: Essays in Criticism* (Atheneum, 1986), pp. 51–84.
2. Ibid., p. 78.
3. W. H. Auden, *Lectures on Shakespeare* (Princeton University Press, 2000), pp. 204–5. When this posthumous book first appeared, it was Tony Hecht who told me I should get it at once.
4. Alan Blyth, *Opera on Record* (Hutchinson, 1979), p. 320.
5. Dyneley Hussey, *Verdi,* second revision (J. M. Dent & Sons, 1963), p. 269.
6. Ibid., p. 278.

III

Falstaff

11

Musical Falstaffs

It will help determine the true stature of Verdi's *Falstaff* if we consider what other composers made of Sir John. Some works about him have been lost or forgotten—by, for instance, Peter Ritter (1764–1841), Karl Ditters von Dittersdorf (1739–1799), and Giovanni Pacini (1796–1867). In listening to those works that are still (at least occasionally) performed, we must first ask which Falstaff is being treated in the music, since many think that there are two different figures under that name in Shakespeare's plays— the outsize figure in the *Henry IV* plays and the diminished one in *The Merry Wives of Windsor*. The critic Harold Bloom, who idolizes the first Falstaff for sharing with Hamlet the title of "Shakespeare's most intelligent character," takes it as a personal insult to him, Bloom, that Shakespeare could so mistreat his hero in *Merry Wives*.[1] Those who deal with Falstaff in music must choose which (if either) of these figures they should present. Some draw only on *Henry IV* (Elgar, Holst), some only on *Merry Wives* (Salieri, Balfe), and some on *Merry Wives* with added material from *Henry IV* (Verdi, Vaughan Williams).

♪ *Salieri* (1799)

All librettists drawing from the plays must reduce the story for the more expansive treatment of music (with arias and ensembles as well as recitatives). The librettist for Salieri's *Falstaff*, a lawyer named Carlo Prospero Defranceschi, made deep cuts. He entirely eliminated the roles of Anne, Fenton, Mistress Quickly, Shallow, Pistol, Nym, Hugh Evans, and Doctor Caius. He changed Mistress Page to Mrs. Slender.

The Falstaff presented here is a numskull, part miles gloriosus, part Tartuffe. The libretto explains his misperception that he is loved by the women, Mrs. Ford and Mrs. Slender (Page), by opening with a ball at Mrs. Slender's home, where Falstaff thinks he is a social hit, though everyone is laughing behind his back. He sings a *brindisi*, then dances minuets with the women, bumping them with his belly.

Back at his inn, Falstaff composes love letters to the women, reading aloud as he writes (the women will not have to read them aloud when they receive them). Bardolfo is comedy's typically grumbling servant, a stock figure from Roman times through the parts Eric Blore played so well in 1930s movies. He refuses to deliver the letters, so a page must do that. Mrs. Slender receives the letter alone in her house, and is so indignant that she sings a vendetta aria against Falstaff. But when Mrs. Ford comes in, she is amused. They compare the letters in a sprightly duet—"La stessa, la stessissima" (The same, the samest)—which Beethoven liked well enough to create a set of piano variations on it.

With Falstaff diminished, Mrs. Ford becomes the towering figure of the opera, the choreographer of responses and the plotter of Falstaff's downfall. She combines with her role elements of the original Mistress Quickly and of Anne. As Quickly, she takes back the answers to Falstaff's letters. But since she cannot do so in her own identity, she disguises herself as a German flirt, whom Falstaff chases around the room. As Anne, she is the object of her husband's impassioned tenor love songs. Like Anne, she summons the fairies in the Herne's Oak scene. All three of Falstaff's humiliations (the laundry basket, disguise as the old woman of Brainford, torture in the forest) are retained, but the defeat of Ford's jealousy is a greater concern than Falstaff's downfall. In the last scene, both Ford and Falstaff have to say they will offend "no more" (*mai più*), the last words of the opera. Falstaff is given no redeeming claim that he causes wit in others.

This is a conventional but well-made eighteenth-century comedy. The music is lovely and varied. Some of it rises—despite the efforts of Pushkin and Shaffer to whittle down Salieri—to Mozartean quality, especially the love songs of Ford, at last responded to by his wife. But despite its many merits, it has been eclipsed by Verdi—as Rossini's *Otello* was dwarfed by Verdi's.

♩ *Balfe* (1838)

The Irishman Michael William Balfe was a musical omnipresence in Victorian England—Sir Thomas Beecham called him "the most interesting British musical figure of the nineteenth century." A prodigy who was composing tunes on the violin for his father's dancing class at age seven, he went on to sing baritone roles in opera, to conduct operas at Her Majesty's Theatre in London, and to compose thirty-eight operas. During a period in Italy, he came to know Rossini and sing in his operas (*Il Barbiere di Siviglia* and *Otello,* among others). Returned to London, he conducted the premieres of Verdi operas (and consulted Verdi when the composer brought *I Masnadieri* to England). As one might expect, his own work imitates Rossini, with harpsichord-accompanied recitatives, aria-cabaletta combinations, patter songs, and insistent crescendos. That is true of his *Falstaff,* revived and recorded by Opera Ireland in 2008.

His earlier operas had been set to English texts, but for *Falstaff* he used an Italian libretto written by Manfredo Maggioni, an Anglo-Italian. For Balfe's opera, the chorus of Windsor busybodies is given a major role. The work opens with Misters Page and Ford berating Falstaff in the street for not repaying loans to them, and the chorus intervenes to break up the quarrel. Falstaff is submitted to all three of the play's humiliations (dunking in the Thames, dressing as a woman, and being antlered in the forest). After his immersion in the Thames he is discovered walking down the street in a muddied condition, where he is forced to explain to the chorus what he underwent. Anne (Annetta) is more prominent than in other versions. Falstaff sends her a letter, along with those to Mrs. Ford and Mrs. Page, complicating the silliness of a multifront wooing.

Surprisingly, there is no bucolic music for the forest scene. Falstaff just meets Mrs. Ford and they sing a sappy love duet to harp arpeggios. Then Falstaff is startled by the arrival not of Meg or the imps, but of Ford as the jealous husband. Falstaff hides in the tree, and is stalked by the chorus. When Falstaff confesses that he is a numskull (*stordito*), the truth of that is all too apparent. Mrs. Ford appropriately ends the opera she has commanded, more interested in rebuking her husband than in paying any more attention to Falstaff. It is a sense of priorities we share.

Nicolai (1849)

Die Lustigen Weiber von Windsor by Otto Nicolai (1810–1849) was rejected by the Vienna Hofoper in 1846, but it was a great success when Nicolai premiered it at the Berlin Staatsoper in 1849. As the only Falstaff opera other than Verdi's to be regularly performed, it is the obvious rival for *Falstaff,* just as Rossini's work was the rival for *Otello.* Balfe, remember, had written operas in English until he used an Italian text for *Falstaff.* Nicolai, by contrast, wrote four Italian operas before setting a German text for *Lustigen Weiber,* a singspiel written by the German-Jewish poet Salomon Hermann Mosenthal.

The opera eliminates Pistol, Bardolf, Shallow, and Mistress Quickly. Hugh Evans with his Welsh accent is likewise jettisoned, but Doctor Cajus is kept, French bumblings and all. Slender, too, is retained so there will be three wooers of Anna. Since Quickly and Pistol are gone, there are no intermediaries calling on Falstaff at the Garter Inn.

Falstaff is not a forceful presence here. The women are in the forefront, and punishing Ford is as important as humbling Falstaff. The lovers, Anna and Fenton, are highlighted in a work that verges on operetta. The thwarting of the suitors Cajus and Slender (Spärlich) is a great part of the fun. The last act is almost Mendelssohnian in its dreamy address to the moon, its songs by Anna and Fenton as Titania and Oberon, and its dances by the elves. Themes from the famous overture are used again, including the gallop, used for the pinching-poking of Falstaff. The mood is pleasant and lighthearted, without the heft of either Shakespeare or Verdi.

Elgar (1913)

Sir Edward Elgar treated Falstaff episodes from *Henry IV* in his *Falstaff,* which he called "a symphonic study." It begins with a lumbering theme for Falstaff, soon crossed by a sweeping one for Prince Hal. The Gads Hill and battle scenes are as much about their rural sites as about active conflict. There are lyrical idylls, especially in the two short interludes where Falstaff dreams of being a slender youth (lovelorn, not sprightly) or lingers in Shallow's orchard. There is no Doll Tearsheet or cowardice in the field. At the end Hal takes the throne (to music like one of Elgar's processionals) and Falstaff's theme dwindles and dies. It is a piece drenched in nostalgia.

⸙ *Holst (1925)*

At the Boar's Head, by Gustav Holst, is a one-act opera setting English songs to texts of *Henry IV*, with a bass Falstaff, a tenor Prince Hal, sopranos for Doll Tearsheet and the Hostess, a tenor Peto, and baritones Bardolph and Pistol. The episodes include the Gads Hill dispute, the mock interview with the king, a battle scene (to patriotic "St. George" music), banter with Doll and the Hostess, and the death of Sir John. At one point Hal sings Shakespeare's Sonnet 12 on time's effects, and Falstaff answers with a time-defying song of jollity. After they have sung separately, they repeat their airs simultaneously, and Doll joins in to make a three-part piece. The best songs are the few composed originally by Holst, especially Hal's soliloquy on why he engages in "wanton" days. As one expects from the material, there is a "Jolly Old England" air to the exercise that treats Falstaff sentimentally.

🎶 *Vaughan Williams (1929)*

Holst's friend Ralph Vaughan Williams did his own version of Falstaff four years after *At the Boar's Head,* this one called *Sir John in Love.* Like Holst, he sets English airs, but he adds more original settings for poems from the sixteenth and seventeenth centuries. He was not intimidated by competition with Verdi, since he thought Boito's libretto put a straitjacket on the composer, leaving little room for Verdi's normally expansive style:

> The real Verdi carried on his drama in terms of broad tunes, but Boito's medicated Shakespeare hardly ever gives him a chance. Again and again the orchestra seems to be preparing us for something like the big tunes of his earlier operas, but then they do not materialize. Let us be grateful, however, for the heavenly melody with the oboe which accompanies the love-making of Anne and Fenton. Here the composer was not hampered by the librettist's sham Shakespeare and was able to rejoice in good Italian slush all about kissing.[2]

Vaughan Williams's opera is nothing if not expansive and leisurely. Like Holst he includes "Interludes," one for choral flower gathering, another for floral crowning of the lovers Anne and Fenton, a third to introduce the Herne's Oak scene with "Greensleeves." Mistress Ford and Falstaff also sing "Greensleeves" to each other. When Falstaff is told that the merry wives await him, instead of issuing a bombastic boast, as in Shakespeare and Verdi, he sings a soupy love song. Perhaps the least plausible of all the musical variations on the Falstaff theme is that of Falstaff as amorous swain.

Outside of Verdi, the only way composers could find to keep Falstaff from being a bumbling idiot (Salieri, Balfe, Nicolai) was to sentimentalize him as a spirit of Ye Olde England (Elgar, Holst, Vaughan Williams). Boito could do better.

Notes

1. Harold Bloom, *Shakespeare: The Invention of the Human* (Riverhead Books, 1998), pp. 271, 315–18.
2. Ralph Vaughan Williams, "Falstaff," *Opera*, February 1951.

12

Falstaff's First Performers

ʔ *Shakespeare's Performers*

KEMP AND BURBAGE

Some consider *The Merry Wives of Windsor* Shakespeare's weakest comedy. It is certainly different from the rest. The only comedy set in England (many of the others used Italian locales), it has the greatest amount of prose (almost 90 percent) as opposed to verse.[1] Its characters, all but Falstaff the knight, are of middle-class status or lower. Though its setting is rural, it has the personnel and language of the "city comedies" of Ben Jonson, Thomas Dekker, and Thomas Middleton. Each outlandish character has his or her own linguistic peculiarities: Pistol's braggadocio, Slender's hiding behind timorous phrases, Nym's verbal tic of "humors," Mistress Quickly's malapropisms, Doctor Caius's fractured French, Hugh Evans's plosive Welshisms. We get an almost Dickensian linguistic stew of slang. As Samuel Johnson wrote:

> This comedy is remarkable for the variety and number of the personages, who exhibit more characters appropriated and discriminated, than perhaps can be found in any other play. Whether Shakespeare was the first that produced upon the English stage the effect of language distorted and depraved by provincial or foreign pronunciation, I cannot certainly decide. . . . Its success must be derived almost wholly from

the players, but its power in a skilful mouth, even he that despises it is unable to resist.[2]

It appears that this showcase of bumpkins was first mouthed for the amusement of an aristocratic audience. The play includes insider court references like the baffled quest of Count Mompelgard for admission to the Order of the Garter.[3]

The idea that the play was for a court performance became fixed in the legend that Queen Elizabeth asked the Lord Chamberlain's Men to show her "Sir John in love." One trouble with that claim is that Shakespeare does not show Falstaff in love. Sir John in the play is angling for the merry wives' money. There is no romance in Shakespeare's Falstaff (as opposed to Vaughan Williams's). To quote Dr. Johnson again: "Falstaff could not love but by ceasing to be Falstaff."[4]

The passage in which the fake "fairies" are told to prepare for the Garter ceremonies at Windsor led to the idea that the play was performed at the ceremony where the company's patron, the Lord Chamberlain George Carey, Lord Hunsdon, became a Knight of the Garter. This took place in 1597, at the St. George Chapel in Windsor, which explains the play's rural setting. But the literary detective Leslie Hotson noted that *Merry Wives* talks of *preparation* for that ceremony, and that the queen did not attend the event in 1597, when the Garter was bestowed on Hunsdon. But she was present at Whitehall Palace in Westminster when Hunsdon was elected to the order, a month before the investiture in Windsor. So Hotson argued that the play was first put on before the queen on St. George's Day, April 23, 1597.[5] That would explain the unusual number of boy actors in the play. Not only did the palace have choristers, but Hunsdon kept his own musical establishment.[6]

If that is the proper date, then claims about nearby plays' dating would put *Merry Wives* between the other treatments of Falstaff, in *1 Henry IV* (winter season of 1596–97) and *2 Henry IV* (winter season of 1597–98). This chronology brings up a famous problem. Why did Shakespeare promise in the Epilogue to Part Two to bring Falstaff back in a play called *Henry V,* which he did not do? He had finished *Merry Wives* while he was writing Part Two, where the Epilogue would say:

> If you be not too much cloy'd with fat meat, our humble author will continue the story, with Sir John in it, and make you merry with fair Katherine of France, where (for anything I know) Falstaff shall die of a sweat, unless already 'a be kill'd with your hard opinions.

Since the Epilogue promises to dance the play-ending jig for them, and Will Kemp was the most famous jig dancer of his time, it is most likely that Kemp himself, stepping out of his role as Falstaff, played the Epilogue. Then why break his own promise to show up again? This was the very time when Kemp was arranging his spectacular morris dance all the way to Norwich, a theatrical stunt that involved elaborate publicity and self-imposed rules (C 2.203, 2.418). He tells us in his book on the dance tour that "I have without good help danced myself out of the World [i.e., the Globe]."[7]

The morris feat shows how strong Kemp was. He had to dance with thick bracelets of bells on his calves through a bog where he sank "over ankles" in mud and then danced on through a snowstorm. Various people tried to join him for short stretches, but dropped out when fatigued. Hosts put him up at inns, mayors came out to greet him, gamblers bet on his failing. The morris was a dance full of energetic leaping, to shake the bells; but though he confesses to getting weary in his pamphlet (*Kemp's Nine Days Wonder*, 1600), he successfully completed the course. He crowned the final steps at Norwich, where the mayor and an orchestra awaited him, by leaping over the wall of the cathedral grounds. The dance became legendary. His shoes were nailed to the wall in tribute to his leap, and a plaque on the wall of St. John Maddermarket still measures the height of his jump.[8]

The power and energy of Kemp help explain how Falstaff can be a force of nature, even though he is "inclining to threescore" and his hair is white (*1 Henry IV*, 2.4.425, 468). But his age is like that of Virgil's Charon, a "raw green ancientness" (*Aeneid* 6.304). In fact, Boito and Verdi criticized the watercolor sketches made for the operatic Falstaff as having too much white hair—he should still have his virility (F 119, 121).

Some people question whether Kemp played Falstaff. Admittedly, he was the leading comic actor in the Lord Chamberlain's Men during the 1590s. But he is normally considered a rustic "clown," not a clever "fool." Since the Folio plays have no cast assignments, and Kemp is specified in entries for only two Quarto roles—Peter in *Romeo and Juliet* and Dogberry in *Much Ado About Nothing*—it was thought he must have specialized in simpletons, which would not equip him to be a witty knight like Falstaff.[9]

But Falstaff's status as knight should not be overdone. He is poor, scrounging for money, ducking his bar tab. He has no family estate—he lives in disreputable inns. His acquaintances, except for the Prince, are riffraff. Even the two figures of minor authority he knows—the country justices Shallow and Silence—

are corrupt nincompoops, as their satirical names indicate. Falstaff has no proud lineage he can refer to. The only references to a past at the Court are Shallow's mention that he was a page to the Duke of Norfolk and that he pummeled the Court jester Scoggin (*2 Henry IV*, 3.2.25, 30). Falstaff does not act like a knight on the battlefield or at Gads Hill. He is a pretentious figure whom Hal humors as a rogue, just like the other riffraff in his company. Dr. Johnson saw that Falstaff's function with the Prince is simply to amuse him, like a jester:

> The man thus corrupt, thus despicable, makes himself necessary to the prince that despises him, by the most pleasing of all qualities, perpetual gaiety, by an unfailing power of exciting laughter, which is the more freely indulged as his wit is not of the splendid or ambitious kind, but consists in easy escapes and sallies of levity, which make sport but raise no envy. It must be observed that he is stained with no enormous or sanguinary crimes so that his licentiousness is not so offensive but that it may be borne for his mirth.[10]

Looked at in this light, the distance between the Falstaff of the comedy and that of the histories is not so great after all. Nor is the distance between Kemp the clown and Kemp the fool very great. Our evidence does not allow us to restrict Kemp to bumpkin roles. He certainly does not write like a bumpkin in *Nine Days Wonder*, where he refers to himself as a fool, never a clown, and he self-consciously plays with words and poses. The most interesting tale of a man who joined his dance for a while refers to the fool of a man at whose house he had stayed. Kemp left the house in foul weather, only to find the fool imitating him: "Mr. Colt's fool would needs dance with me, and had his desire where, leaving me, two fools parted fair in a foul way."[11] That sounds less like Dogberry than like Touchstone dealing with William.

If Kemp had the lead role in this play, what was left for the troupe's star and main attraction, Richard Burbage? The role of Ford deepens the comedy with his jealousy, reminiscent of Othello's. This is the most prominent part after Falstaff's—304 lines to Kemp's 424. In the nineteenth century, leading actor-producers have taken the part of Ford—Edmund Kean, for instance, and John Philip Kemble.[12] In Verdi's opera, the role of Ford has sometimes been a star maker, as when Lawrence Tibbett stepped into the role in 1925 at the Met.

Ford's role gave Burbage plenty of scope for his skills, and his playing it would have given the whole play extra resonance. The interplay between Kemp and Burbage, already explored in the *Henry* plays where Burbage played Hal to Kemp's Falstaff, would have given *Merry Wives* more stature than some later critics allow it. The bustling scenes of search for Falstaff take dramatic range. As Verdi wrote of the character in his opera, Ford, "in a towering outburst of jealousy, roars, screams, jumps all over, etc." (F 207). The part demands energy, intensity, and plausibility, all of which were marks of the Burbage range.

⸮ *Verdi's Performers*

MAUREL, PASQUA, ZILLI, PINI-CORSI

Boito and Ricordi found it easier to draw Verdi into composing *Falstaff* than into *Otello*. Yet Verdi knew that this last effort could fail if he did not find the right cast. Even when he had lined up some of his singers, he worried that they could not be trained for the new kind of opera he meant to create—one of quicksilvery alterations, precise and witty singing, and scintillating orchestral effects. He wrote to Ricordi:

> You see how hard it will be to find all that is necessary. I add that the piano and stage rehearsals will be long, because it will not be easy to perform it as I want—and I will be very demanding, and not as I was for *Otello,* where, out of regard for this or that person [e.g., favoring Faccio's mistress], and to pose as a serious, worthy, and venerable man, I endured everything. No, no, I shall again be the bear of old, and all of us will benefit from it. . . . The music is not difficult, but will have to be sung differently from other modern operas. I would not want it to be sung, for example, like *Carmen,* and not even like *Don Pasquale* or [Ricci's] *Crispino.* There is need for study, and that will take time. Our singers, in general, can only sing with big voices; they have neither vocal flexibility nor clear and easy diction, and they lack phrasing and breath. (F 208)

Verdi's search for the right cast should have been eased by the fact that he knew from the outset who should be the most important performer. For Falstaff he wanted Victor Maurel, the Jago of his *Otello.* But Maurel threw up a roadblock that almost ended the project. He created a list of demands and had his wife, Anne, take them to Ricordi for inclusion in his contract: four thousand francs per performance, ten thousand francs for rehearsal sessions, sixteen thousand francs to be sent to Paris right away, a new dressing room built for him, and the right to be the first Falstaff in all the major theaters of Europe and North America (as if the managers of those theaters would have no say in how they hired their lead singer) (F 242).

Verdi exploded. He wrote to Ricordi:

> In this morning's telegram I told you, "Cancel everything!"
> I now repeat the same words. "Cancel everything," not one
> time, but twenty! . . . In dangerous matters the worst thing
> is hesitation! Here we must not hesitate, but publish Maurel's
> pretensions at once, and also my telegram, and add "there-
> fore *Falstaff* cannot be performed." (F 241)

To blame Maurel in the papers for sabotaging the last work of Italy's most beloved composer was certainly playing a high-stakes game, but Verdi was never slow to reject compromises. He showed his anger in more detail in his follow-up letter to Ricordi:

> Do not hesitate to break off all negotiations. My self-respect
> is too offended by Maurel's proposals. Imagine! A singer,
> whoever he may be, comes to my study to take possession
> of my not-yet-completed opera, saying, "I will perform your
> opera, but afterwards I want to be the first performer in the
> leading theatres . . . London, Madrid, etc. . . . I do not accept
> the 10,000 lire for the rehearsal, either!! *C'est trop fort!* What
> a precedent. . . . This is terrible. Enough, though. Do not
> waste time. Break off everything!! I give myself leave, after
> all, to still be the owner of my opera! *I firmly declare that I can-
> not accept, nor do I accept, any of Maurel's proposals.* (F 244–45)

Ricordi telegraphed back: "I DECLARE ALL NEGOTIATIONS SUS-
PENDED AND CUT OFF" (F 247). Verdi had to repeat his angry refus-
als, spelling out *his* conditions:

1. There is no obligation to give *Falstaff* where it suits others.
2. There will be no exorbitant fees for the artists.
3. There will be no paid rehearsals. . . .

If I were faced with the dilemma of either accepting these terms or burning the score, then I would light the fire at once, and I would lay Falstaff and his belly on the funeral pyre myself. (F 247–48)

Ricordi sent a copy of this letter to Maurel at Aix-les-Bains, and Maurel replied with a panicky telegram regretting "SERIOUS MISUNDERSTANDING," telling Ricordi he was leaving that very day to see Verdi at his home at Sant'Agata (F 52).

But Madame Maurel was still holding out. She sent Verdi a letter saying she had settled with Luigi Piontelli (the manager of La Scala) for forty performances by Maurel "in three and a half months at La Scala, Rome, Florence, etc." Verdi fumed:

If this is true [that Piontelli had made such a deal], I have nothing more to tell you except to return the 1st act of *Falstaff* and not to talk about it again. . . . I shall never, never, never accept these conditions. I told you from the beginning in a telegram that I would never pass under these *Caudine Forks*. (F 252)

(The Caudine Forks is a reference to the Apulian pass where Samnites defeated a Roman army in 321 BCE and forced the surviving Romans to file out under a yoke.)

Madame Maurel now claimed that she never thought Verdi, who "lives in the starry heavens of his artistic dreams," would have been bothered by mere details of business. She blamed

Ricordi for forwarding her conditions to the composer—she was hoping to sneak the extravagant terms around the famously prickly maestro (F 253). It was left for Maurel himself to capitulate, signing his contract on Ricordi's (and Verdi's) terms (F 254). When Verdi finally got Maurel to rehearsals, he emphasized the same virtues he had found in the man's Jago—precise articulation of Boito's brilliant words, stage presence, and subtle variation of dynamics.

The singer who, after Maurel, satisfied Verdi most was the mezzo singing the part of Mistress Quickly. He was still searching for the right singer after he rejected Guerrina Fabbri, whom Boito and Ricordi had both recommended (F 210):

> Fabbri, with her lovely, agile voice, can be successful in cantabile pieces such as *La Cenerentola,* etc., etc. But the part of Quickly is something else. It calls for singing and acting, much aplomb on the stage, and the right emphasis in her diction. She does not have these qualities, and we run the risk of sacrificing a part which is the most individual and original one of the four [women]. (F 207)

Next he considered Giuseppina Pasqua, a former soprano turned mezzo who had satisfied him as Eboli in his 1884 revision of *Don Carlo.* But someone said she had aged since then (she was thirty-seven in 1892). He prompted Ricordi to ask Puccini how she was performing for him (in *Edgar* at Ferrara). The younger composer praised her, but Verdi feared it might be for the wrong reasons, so far as Quickly was concerned (F 182). As he wrote to Ricordi:

> Pasqua, according to Puccini's report, is frightening; nevertheless, could you write her and tell her plainly that here the

chips are down, and to dispense with the sentimentality. It is a comedy, no cantabile music, notes and words, bustling about the stage, and lots of vivacity. (F 215)

Ricordi doubted that Pasqua's voice was low enough to "function as the double-bass in the [female] ensembles" (F 220). But Verdi found, in coaching her, that the comic emissary scene with Falstaff was funny enough for him to write a new aria for her to reenact that scene when reporting it to the other women (F 217–18).

A more important part than Quickly is that of Alice Ford. She is the ringleader of the women, the opposite pole from the lumbering Falstaff, the engineer of his downfall. In Verdi's words: "She must be full of the devil. *She stirs the brew*" (F 207). Alice sings what is, in effect, the creed of the merry wives: "Gaie comari di Windsor"—Mirthful Conspirers of Windsor. Verdi chose for Alice the twenty-nine-year-old Emma Zilli, a brilliant singer who would die prematurely of yellow fever on a Latin American tour in 1901. "Zilli, precisely because she is a dramatic artist, will manage to do well in her role, the most brilliant of all" (F 324). But eventually, after letting her sing in the premiere, he decided that Zilli did not meet his high standards of crisp diction and comic energy. He advised Ricordi to seek a replacement for her in the tour of *Falstaff*:

Zilli, who has much talent and who understands and acts well, does not have the flexible voice, however, or the free and easy deportment for that part. She is good, I repeat, but she does not render the part with the brio that is needed, as I also told you, if you recall, at the rehearsals in Milan. Alice is the most important part after Falstaff. For *Falstaff,* do not meddle with artists who want to sing too much and express feeling and action by falling asleep on the notes. (F 427)

The second most important male part in *Falstaff* is that of Ford. Verdi rejected Arturo Pessina for the role:

Pessina is a good artist, but more a singer than actor, and he is a bit stodgy for the part of Ford, who, in a towering outburst of jealousy, roars, screams, jumps all over. . . . Without that, the finale of the second act [the basket scene] would be sacrificed. All the attention is turned to him and to Falstaff's face bumping up and down in the basket. In this part, [Antonio] Pini-Corsi would be better, if his [bow]legs could be fixed. (F 207)

Pini-Corsi, who had just appeared at La Scala as Rigoletto, became Ford, to Verdi's entire satisfaction. His bustling about in the basket scene, bowlegs and all, drew on his extensive experience as a *buffo cantante* in Rossini comedies (bits of which he recorded in the first years of the twentieth century).

Verdi was satisfied with his Nannetta, Shakespeare's Anne Page (Adelina Stehle), and with Meg, Mistress Page (Virginia Guerrini), but he worried about the diction and intonation of his Fenton (Edoardo Garbin). At one rehearsal, a sore throat kept Verdi from demonstrating what effects he wanted Garbin to achieve, and he felt that Garbin was not studying hard enough (F 301). But Verdi's intense coaching kept the cast alert. In over sixty rehearsals, he concentrated on everything, down to the pronunciation of every word. He said the piccolo should be louder in the final fugue, and remarked of the basket scene:

The finale always pianissimo except for the phrase *Voi sarete l'ala destra;* then the rest ppp, always less *marcato;* then the first time for *affogo, affogo* and I would like to see Falstaff's snout come out for the first time.[13]

This was Verdi's last chance at getting an opera right, and he would miss no element in bringing off the coup.

Notes

1. Brian Vickers, *The Artistry of Shakespeare's Prose* (Routledge, 1968), pp. 141–42, 433.
2. *Johnson on Shakespeare,* edited by Arthur Sherbo (Yale University Press, 1968), p. 341.
3. Leslie Hotson, *Shakespeare Versus Shallow* (Nonesuch Press, 1931), pp. 113–15.
4. *Johnson,* op. cit., p. 341.
5. Hotson, op. cit., pp. 115–22.
6. Ibid., p. 120.
7. Will Kemp, *Kemp's Nine Days Wonder* (Johnason Reprint, 1972), p. 3.
8. David Wiles, *Shakespeare's Clown* (Cambridge University Press, 1987), p. 224.
9. There may be another reference to Kemp in the false stage direction of the quarto *2 Henry IV,* 2.4.18, "Enter Will." See Wiles, op. cit., p. 118.
10. *Johnson,* op. cit., p. 523. See Wiles, op. cit., p. 118.
11. Kemp, op. cit., p. 12.
12. H. J. Oliver, *The Merry Wives of Windsor* (Arden Shakespeare, 1971), p. xii.
13. James A. Hepokoski, *Giuseppe Verdi "Falstaff"* (Cambridge University Press, 1983), p. 125.

Inflation

Unlike all others who adapted Falstaff for musical purpose, Boito realized the size of his task. It was not enough to extract Falstaff from the dense layers of the history plays where he appears, nor to accept the ninnification of him in *Merry Wives*. Boito knew that bringing the spirit of Falstaff over from the history plays into the plot of *Merry Wives* called for the creation of an entirely new play, compounded of many elements. He went back to what he considered the source of *Merry Wives*, *Il Pecorone* by Giovanni Fiorentino, and to cognate stories in the *Decameron*—much of whose vocabulary he borrowed (F 363). He added atmosphere from *A Midsummer Night's Dream*. He remixed all these elements in the crucible of his own practiced stagecraft. He was not foolhardy in weighing the complexities of his assignment. He pondered the nature of comedy, the problem of fading interest as the plot is untangled, how to avoid what seemed the inevitable letdown toward the end (F 4). He wrote Verdi at the outset:

> During the first few days I was in despair. To sketch the characters in a few strokes, to weave the plot, to extract all the juice from that enormous Shakespearean pomegranate, without letting useless pits ripple into the little glass; to write colorfully, clearly and briefly; to outline the musical plan of the scene so that an organic unity may result that should and yet should not be "a piece of music"; to make the

merry comedy live from beginning to end, to make it live with natural and communicative cheer is difficult, difficult, difficult; but it must seem easy, easy, easy. (F 16–17)

Like all who adapt a play for opera purposes, Boito had to begin by streamlining the plot, eliminating minor characters—Hugh Evans, Shallow, Slender, Simple. One of the three humiliations of Falstaff (dressing him as the Brainford woman) is dismissed. Verdi initially wanted to cut out the marriages at the end; but Boito rightly insisted that they be retained (B 3.425)—the confused identities of bride and groom, the mixture of fake marriage and real love, are too much a part of the omnidirectional foolery of the work. Verdi was shying away from the temptation that other composers fall into when setting *Merry Wives*—to expand the love story of Anne and Fenton in conventional operatic terms, with extended love duets. Boito assured him that he had a solution for that problem:

This amorous play between Nannetta and Fenton must appear in very frequent spurts; in all the scenes where they are present they will steal kisses hidden in corners, slyly, boldly, without letting themselves be discovered, with fresh little phrases and short little dialogues, very rapid and cunning from the beginning to the end of the opera. It will be a most cheerful love, always disturbed and interrupted, and always ready to begin again. This color, which is good, must not be forgotten. (F 5)

Without realizing it, Boito had predicted the *tinta* of the whole opera, its touch-and-go teasing quality, its jolly air of chaos. This is just the way Verdi was foreseeing the work. He quickly started on a comic fugue, not even knowing where or why it would figure in the plot, only that "it may go well in *Falstaff*" (F 15). He wondered how it could be identified as comic without, as yet, having comic words. "Why comic, you will say. I don't know how, or why, but it is a comic fugue." Boito found just the right place for the fugue, at the end, and the right words for it, to express the spirit of the entire opera:

> Tutto nel mondo è burla.
> L'uom è nato burlone,
> Nel suo cervello ciurla
> Sempre la sua ragione.
> Tutti gabbàti. . . .
> [Life's nothing but a mocking.
> Each man is framed for clowning.
> Dizzy in his head flickers
> What stuff he takes for thinking.
> All fall to con men. . . .]

(*Gabbare* is to cheat or swindle; so *gabbàti* are the cheated or conned.)

Boito would keep making his lovers the model for other aspects of the work:

> I like their love; it serves to refresh and solidify the entire comedy. That love must enliven each and every thing, and always in such a way that I would almost skip the duet of the two lovers. . . . It is useless to let the two of them just sing together in a real duet. Even without the duet that part will be very effective; it will be even more effective without it. I cannot explain myself; I would like, as sugar is sprinkled on

a cake, to sprinkle the whole comedy with their merry love without accumulating it at any point. (F 11)

Boito followed this line of thought to the point of suggesting that Fenton not be given any set aria at all (F 5). But he and Verdi thought better of this idea. Boito composed a brilliant sonnet for the aria, and Verdi took special pains in coaching Garbin to sing it.

The finished work shows how perfectly Boito and Verdi had grasped its spirit from the outset. As Dyneley Hussey puts it:

The melody is recognizably the melody of Verdi, but it comes now in brief snatches that elude the ear, and make the listener wish to call the music to halt in its swift passage, that he may examine and appreciate to the full its fleeting beauty. For not only have the long melodies—square-cut to an eight-bar pattern that could be seized at once by the memory and carried away from the opera house—given way to a more subtle and, as it were, kaleidoscopic style, but the tunes no longer begin and end with an obvious signal; they tend to melt into one another, and the distinction between them and recitative has grown so faint that the music becomes a continuous arioso. The melodic ideas dissolve and reshape themselves in new forms, with a swiftness that leaves even the most athletic brain forever panting at their heels. For this reason there is really nothing that can be lifted from *Falstaff* for performance in the concert hall, though baritones do occasionally show off their command of patter by singing *Quando ero paggio*. And that very exception gives a measure of the diminutive scale of the component parts of the opera. It is all over in a few seconds. . . . [*Falstaff*] is seen to be not merely swift and compact but of the lightest imaginable specific gravity.[1]

One can argue with an aspect of that last sentence. There is one aspect of the opera that has heavy specific gravity—the unwieldy weight of Falstaff himself. But it is true that the effect of the whole work is to puncture and toss in the air and sink Falstaff. In fact, what keeps the opera from splintering into brilliant fragments (which is what Vaughan Williams called it) is the large structural concept that binds together all its parts. The musical shape of the thing is wonderfully clear. On the one hand we have the staggering pomposity of Falstaff, a bloated swagger, slow and self-assured—an inflation of the protagonist's importance. Against that is pitted the light and skittering assault troop of three women, swiftly puncturing the Pancione. And blundering between these two poles are the blind and angry four men. Soaring over all this turmoil and confusion is the sweet bantering of Fenton and Nannetta.

Verdi is endlessly inventive in varying these components. Just when it seems he has exhausted all expedients, he and Boito come up with the miraculous third act. They drove the action pell-mell to the climax of the basket scene ending Act 2, and they feared the last act would be an inevitable letdown. Instead, like a magician saving his best illusion for last, they gave a whole new spiritual dimension to the conclusion.

The Falstaff of Shakespeare's *Merry Wives* is not a formidable adversary. He is too easily made the butt of other people's jokes. Boito helped even the balance by taking out the Lady of Brainford trick. But he also fortified the image of Falstaff with lines and scenes from the *Henry IV* plays. The most commonly recognized borrowings are the honor monologue in Act 1 and memories of Falstaff's court life as a page in Act 2. But Hepokoski shows how constant and clever are the many little quotations from the histories.[2] Verdi's first task is to make Falstaff a worthy target for the merry wives—not only fat and obvious, but dominating and important. That is what the first scene does. Verdi's music gives Falstaff a stature that he lacked in *Merry Wives*. As Verdi gave cosmic reach to *Otello*'s music, he turns Falstaff into a force of nature, an earth-daimon.

The opera begins, as *Otello* had, with a storm of sound. No overture, no lead-in—we plunge at once into a tempest of activity. This may be a tempest in a teapot, but it rattles all the drinking pots at the inn. There is an off-beat chord that acts like a trip wire for the second chord's explosion, like a synco-pated Ah-CHOO. This is not an apocalyptic storm but a psychic detonation—Doctor Cajus erupting over Falstaff's assaults on his person, his property, his livestock—"not, remember, your house-maid," Falstaff casually adds to the sputtering list. (Bryn Terfel gets a sly smile into his delivery of the line in the Abbado record-ing.) Cajus fumes back: "Such a favor!—my bleary-eyed old hag!"

As Cajus fizzes on, Falstaff flings him an admission as if dis-tributing alms: "Here is what I have to say: I did all that you mention" (rising inflection of conceding)—"and meant to do it" (falling dismissal). Cajus is deferential even in his anger. He calls Falstaff *"Ampio Messere"* (Outsize persona) and says he would per-sist even if his adversary were "Sir John twenty times over." The Doctor says he will take Falstaff to the Royal Council. Falstaff dismisses his threat with a pun on "Council" and "Counsel"—as if Cajus said, "This will be treated in court," and Falstaff yawns that it will get "curt treatment." Boito fills this scene with puns and quirk-rhymes (*favola/tavola, lanterna/taverna*). When Falstaff tells Bardolfo and Pistola to answer the Doctor's accusations, Cajus and Pistola shout at each other in an exchange like the ancient insult contests called flytings. Boito fits these rapid-fire exchanges into his basic fourteener verses:

"Yokel!"
 "Nut!"
"Sponger!"
 "Beast!"
"Cur!"
 "Dregs!"
"Straw man!"
 "Midget!"
"Mandrake root!"
 "Who?"
"You!"
 "Say again?"
"Right!"
 "Devil!"

Falstaff ends the contest by punning on Pistola's name: "Pistol, don't fire yourself here." After having let the dispute boil all around him, Falstaff at last pronounces his verdict, half in the tone of a judge, half in that of a divine: "The charges are refuted. Pass on in peace now." Cajus, taking up the pastoral note, swears to ecclesiastical trombones that he will never get drunk again except with the godly.

At this Bardolfo and Pistola chant a rough canon, *"Ah-ah-ah-men!"* but Bardolfo is too slow. Falstaff growls: "Break off this counterpoint—you bark it out of tempo." Falstaff is thinking in a pun: *rubato,* a "stealing," is the musical term for stealing time out of a phrase. He goes on: "Art preserves this supreme maxim: Robbing [*rubar*] needs graceful timing. You are disgraceful artists." Boito's lightning play of ideas has Falstaff letting the two men off for stealing from Cajus's pocket, but reflecting on their clumsiness when he hauls them before the bar for stealing time from a musical phrase.[3]

When Cajus leaves, the innkeeper gives Falstaff his bill. As Falstaff savors in memory the "one anchovy" on it, he tells Bardolfo to search his purse. When the search is fruitless, Falstaff sings a neat little meandering tune about wandering from tavern to tavern, with Bardolfo's inflamed nose as his lantern. It is a sweet and rather fond moment, tossed off lightly. Spike Hughes says of it: "That Verdi could use these eight bars here and then forget them for good and all is maddeningly characteristic of the lavishness of invention in this opera—and, incidentally, the sort of thing which makes Falstaff the most difficult of his operas to analyze and quote from."[4] Then, in a succession of quick changes in mood, Falstaff says that his two subordinates are draining his money and his very flesh. What he saves in lamp oil by using Bardolfo's nose to light his way he wastes in wine to fuel that nasal fire. In a phrase of wistful self-pity, he sings: "If Falstaff should get thinner, he is not *he*—no longer loved." Then in the grandest manifesto manner: "In this abdomen is my dominion, proclaimed by a thousand tongues." His lackeys trumpet as to their emperor:

> Falstaff Immenso!
>   Enorme Falstaff!
> [Falstaff the Grand!
>   Outsize Falstaff!]

He nods triumphantly. "Here is my realm, what I augment."
When the lackeys refuse to deliver his love letters, Bardolfo saying that honor forbids him, Boito introduces the honor catechism from 1 *Henry IV* (5.1.131–41). Falstaff in the play ticks off, on the battlefield, the reasons he will not risk his life in com-

bat. Here, Falstaff says that his two flunkies are too scurvy to have honor: *"L'onore! Ladri . . . cloache d'ignominia!"* (Honor? You lowlifes . . . sewers of filth). J. B. Steane admired the way Toscanini's Falstaff, Mariano Stabile, delivered these lines: "The crescendo on the first syllable of *ladri* culminates in a gruff-voiced menace on the second syllable, vivid as a fist shaken in the face."[5] Stabile also richly rolls off the phrase *"Può l'onore r-r-riempir-r-rvi la pancia?"* (Can honor r-r-r-enr-r-r-ich paunch lining?). Then the considered pauses before each "no" added to the catalog show a finicky skill at accounting.

Falstaff makes a surprising admission that he himself, "I, even I," cannot always afford honor, but hides that fact from the face of God. The effrontery is amusing, but Falstaff is showing that it is hard for him to keep his dignity in the low company and the low inn where he has ended up. This is a side of Falstaff that is not often shown in modern performances, where cheap laughs are sought by making Falstaff a ninny. Anthony Tommasini, that fine critic, has a different take on the character. Praising Geraint Evans's interpretation, he writes:

> The opera only works on the resonant level Verdi intended if Falstaff is portrayed as more than some risible has-been. Long the butt of jokes, he carries around a bellyful of resentments. A great Falstaff must dare to convey the character's darkness and simmering anger, while still making him the kind of irascible charmer you'd like to have a beer with.[6]

After an interlude in which the women get and read Falstaff's identical love letters and plot their revenge, in Act 2 Pistola and

Bardolfo return to the inn chanting their repentance, with an *acciaccatura* over the fourth syllable:

> Siam penti-EE-ti!
> E contri-EE-ti!
> [We're repeh-EHN-ting!
> Not conteh-EHN-ding!]

They are feigning. They are really there to introduce Mistress Quickly, who will spring the merry women's trap. This is the comic scene that Verdi chose Giuseppina Pasqua to perform. She begins with an elaborate bow, addressing Falstaff with an *acciaccatura*:

> Revere-EHN-za!
> Revere-EHN-za!
> [Your High Worth-EE-ness!
> Your High Worth-EE-ness!]

When Quickly tells him how the "poor ladies" are pining for him, modern Falstaffs tend to preen coyly, not allowing their character any dignity at all. But the humor is all in the music and needs no mugging or slapstick to nudge it along. We should remember that Verdi did not want Violetta to cough, Riccardo to laugh, or Jago to sneer. He looked down on extramusical expression.

Similarly, when Ford comes and praises Falstaff's prowess with the women, and offers him money to seduce Alice Ford, Falstaff is made to grab greedily at the gold. And when Falstaff goes off to "make myself pretty," most performers come back in ridiculous popinjay costume, like Osric preening before Hamlet. But Ford's worries must have some basis for his plot to work. There is some trace of the old buck left in Falstaff, enough for the women to work hard to bring him down. The costume and makeup in modern productions go against Boito and Verdi's efforts to give him dignity. Remember that Verdi did not want him to be too old and white haired. Yet the typical modern Falstaff is made up to look almost bald, with thinning white hair.

Franco Zeffirelli's direction of the opera for the Met had Falstaff leaping around frenetically in the first scene, pulling Bardolfo's nose and poking at Pistola during the honor monologue. Falstaff should have an easy air of command, shown in his nonchalant brushing off of Cajus's spluttering. When Falstaff finally does rise in his wrath and chase the two morons with a broom, it should come as an eruption from some volcano thought to be extinct.

Similarly, in the next scene, when Falstaff is wooing Alice, he should not be played as a simpering poseur but with a suavity that lends some plausibility to Alice's feigning a smitten state. In recalling his days of gallantry, Falstaff sings, "When serving as the Duke of Norfolk's page, I was a thin thing, a thin thing, a thin thing" (*ero sottile, sottile, sottile*). In Maurel's recording of the middle phrases, he struts up the first part of the lines, then lightly curtsies back as on tiptoe in the second part (where Verdi marked all the notes staccato):

QUELLO ERA IL TEMPO
del mio verde Aprile
QUELLO ERA IL TEMPO
del mio lieto Maggio.
[THAT WAS THE PERIOD
of my blossomed April
THAT WAS THE PERIOD
of my skipping Maytime.]

Falstaff's polish and poise should not be confined to this short burst of musical sunshine, but should spread through all his wooing. The comic geniuses knew enough to let their funnymen retain some dignity. In Dickens, Wilkins Micawber is in many ways a silly old fellow, but he retains enough moral weight to bring down Uriah Heep. Falstaff must be well and truly inflated before he can be deflated. And then he must have reserves of strength enough to bounce back and lead the laughter of all the others in the end.

Notes

1. Dyneley Hussey, *Verdi,* second revised edition (J. M. Dent & Sons, 1963), pp. 291–92.
2. James A. Hepokoski, *Giuseppe Verdi "Falstaff"* (Cambridge University Press, 1983), pp. 26–29.
3. In *Merry Wives* (1.3.24–28), Falstaff turns Bardolph over to the innkeeper as a tapster, for which he is better suited than for thieving. He says: "his thefts were too open; his filching was like an unskillful singer, he kept not time," and Nym adds, "The good humor is to steal at a minute's rest." Boito could give more edge to the joke because of Italian *rubar/rubato,* and by having Bardolfo actually sing off-time.
4. Spike Hughes, *Famous Verdi Operas* (Chilton Book Company, 1968), p. 485.
5. J. B. Steane, *The Grand Tradition: Seventy Years of Singing on Record*, second edition (Amadeus Press, 1993), p. 185.
6. Anthony Tommasini, *The New York Times Essential Library of Opera* (Times Books, 2004), p. 265.

14
Deflation

If the opening scenes with Falstaff were all swagger and pomp, the scenes with the merry women are feather-light, agile-witted, and nimble of foot. Meg and her friend Mistress Quickly arrive at the Fords' house just as Alice and her daughter, Nannetta, are coming out into the garden. In Shakespeare's play, Mistress Quickly was a servant to Doctor Caius, and slow-witted (making her name an anomaly). Here she is just a friend to the two wives, and as sharp as they. The two wives jokingly say each could be a knight's lady, and they produce their letters to prove it.

As they begin to read, a rather droopy melody in the English horn suggests a lovelorn Falstaff. Hepokoski writes: "A triplet sigh leads to a gentle descent and thence to a concluding note awkwardly beyond the lower limit of the instrument—the final tonic has to be supplied by a clarinet, which thus without warning alters the mood established by the English-horn timbre."[1] We are subtly told that Falstaff is wooing beyond his reach. The first letter to be read begins grandly: *"Fulgida Alice!"* (Far-shining Alice!). The grandiosity is undercut when Falstaff uses the nickname for Margaret: *"Fulgida Meg!"* (Far-shining MEG!). The wives discover that the letters are identical: *"È tal e quale"* (Same here, same there). Falstaff waxes poetic in his sign-off to each letter. Alice reads it with a trill in the plunging last word:

E il viso tuo su me risplenderà
Come una stella sull'imeh-EH-EHN-sità.
[Your face will glitter above me
Like a star above the immeh-EH-EHNSE-ness.]

Alice later sings this in a deflationary way that shows what she thinks of Falstaff's "immenseness." In mock indignation, the wives call Falstaff *"Mostro! Mostro!"* (Weirdo! Weirdo!). And they quickly conclude, *"Dobbiam gabbarlo!"* (We've got to con him!)—an anticipation of the chant at the end of the opera: *"Tutti gabbàti!"* (All fall to con men). The women gloat over what they will do to him in an unaccompanied quartet. Verdi labored over this, and chose his Alice so she could keep the rest on pitch. With later casts, he let a conductor add minimal support from oboe and clarinets if the singers needed it (B 3.461). But he was proud of the bare bubbling up of innocent malice, and let this be one of the two bits encored at the premiere (the other was "Quand'ero paggio" in Act 2). The women are having fun.

Five men enter—Nannetta's young lover Fenton, the aggrieved men Doctor Cajus and Ford, the provocateurs Pistola and Bardolfo. They sing in 4/4 time what Budden calls a kind of "chaotic canon":

All Ford can make of this is "a buzzing of wasps and a humming of angry hornets and a rumbling of storm-bellied clouds," and if these words too are unintelligible, their meaning is brought out by onomatopoeia: a chromatic motif on voices and wind rising and falling twice in pitch and volume and backed by buzzing strings. (B 3.462–63)

The men are not in the same intellectual league with the women. (Barbara Gaines, the director of the Chicago Shakespeare Theater, says Shakespeare's women are typically smarter than men.)

Francis Toye describes the overlap of the male and female companies:

> With the entrance of the men the predominant rhythm changes to 2/2, though the women still cling to their 6/8, the resulting nonet being not only one of the most brilliant things in the opera but one of the most brilliant things ever written. Generically a descendant of the ensembles of Cimarosa and Pergolesi, it looks exceedingly complicated on paper, but in performance it sounds crystal clear.[2]

Fenton breaks off for a first hastily snatched kiss of Nannetta. She sings *"Labbra di foco,"* and he answers, *"Labbra di fiore"* (Fiery lips! Flowery lips!). He ends the brief exchange with a line from Boccaccio, and she continues it:

> Bocca baciata non perde ventura . . .
> . . . anzi rinnova come fa la luna.
> [Kissed lips forfeit not what is to come . . .
> . . . they re-arise, a returning moon.]

When the women and men return, the women still sing to their dancing 6/8 measure, the men plodding on in common time, a tour de force to which Verdi adds, as a crowning touch, the arc of the lovers' lyrical song thrown over the whole. When the men leave, the women contemplate what they are about to do to Falstaff: "You will see that horrid proud belly blimp up, and up, and *up*, and *up*, then—BIG BURST" (si *gonfia*, si *gonfia*, si *gonfia*, si *gonfia, si gonfia,* e poi CREPA). Trombones and bassoons blare in a downward rush as the deflation brings Falstaff's balloon crashing to the ground. The women have put the whole opera in a nutshell.

The scene where Falstaff is deflated follows on Mistress Quickly's embassy to Falstaff. In Act 2 she recounts what she did there, in the aria specially written to milk the scene again, with Quickly mimicking the pompous Falstaff: *"Giunta all'Albergo della Giarrettiera"* (Joining him inside the Garter Inn). Then Alice gives her ringleader's scampering exhortation to the troops:

> Gaie comari di Windsor, è l'ora!
> L'ora d'alzar la risata sonora,
> L'alta risata che scoppia, che scherza,
> Che sfolgora, armata di dardi e di sferza,
> Gaie comari, festosa brigata!
> Sul lieto viso spunti il sorriso,
> Splenda del riso l'acuto fulgor,
> Favilla incendiaria
> Di gioia nell'aria, di gioia nel cor!
> [Merry conspirers of Windsor, let's go!
> Let's loose the rippling laughter,
> A laughter that punctures,
> That dances, that lightnings,
> That wields satire-darts and whips.
> Merry conspirers, you jolly ranks,
> Sharpen the smiles on your face,
> With lightnings that play there,
> An incendiary spark
> To ignite the sky, and the heart!]

Deflation

That program is fulfilled in the second part of Act 2, where at first the fake love music of Falstaff and Alice is played off against the real love music of Fenton and Nannetta. Ford and his posse break in looking for Falstaff to a *moto perpetuo* scurrying figure— the pace is as slaphappy as that of a Marx Brothers picture. When Falstaff first ducks behind the screen, then dives into the clothes basket, and Fenton and Nannetta take his place behind the screen, the suggestion is of a Feydeau farce, with Falstaff's head popping out of the basket to protest that he is being suffocated by the laundry. Just when the pace is getting too frenetic, Boito and Verdi slow it down to the comic stalking of a nonexistent Falstaff behind the screen. To slower rhythms, the three elements of the scene interweave their separate musics—the lyrical lovers, the softly padding male stalkers, the amused observing women, with punctuating cries from the basket. The scene ends with Falstaff being dumped into the Thames.

The act that deflates Falstaff is his inundation. But we do not see him truly deflated until the opening of Act 3. This begins with an orchestral replay of the *moto perpetuo* of his pursuers, as if he were reliving the panic of that scene in his mind. The theme begins softly as a mere memory, then builds to a thunderous repetitiveness as if hammering Falstaff's humiliation into his brain (the drum blows in Toscanini's 1937 recording are like nails in Falstaff's coffin). A soggy and dispirited Falstaff—having floated to shore, he says, only thanks to his belly's buoyancy— croaks like a bloated frog over his plight and the general vileness of the universe (*"Mondo ladro"*). The cocky striding of his earlier self-encouragement—*"Va vecchio John, va, va per la tua via"* (Off, then, old John, pace out your path)—is reprised in a minor key and to the rhythms of a dolorous death march. Only when the innkeeper brings him wine do things begin to brighten. As the blood begins to course again in his body, the music enacts this reanimation. Rippling violins at first imitate the pouring of the wine. Then, in a crescendo of trills, life passes out from a renewed Falstaff into a scintillating cosmos. Boito's words and Verdi's music present this miraculous resurrection:

> Ber del vin dolce e sbottonarsi al sole
> Dolce cosa! Il buon vino sperde le tetre fole
> Dello sconforto, accende l'occhio e il pensier, dal labbro
> Sale al cervel e quivi risveglia il picciol fabbro
> Dei trilli, un negro grillo che vibra entro l'uom brillo.
> Trilla ogni fibra in cor, l'allegro etere al trillo
> Guizza e il giocondo globo squilibra una demenza
> Trillante! E il trillo invade il mondo!
> [To sip sweet wine and bask in the sun
> How sweet! Good wine dispels
> Depression. It lights up eye and mind,
> It swirls from lip to brain, where it awakens
> The busy little trillings of the cricket
> That sings in the drinker.
> Every heartstring thrills,
> The happy air quivers, the globe reels
> In a frenzy of trills. THE UNIVERSE IS TRILLING.]

Budden writes of the effect:

The musical illustration of the trill is one of Verdi's most famous orchestral tours de force. Starting on the second flute, while first and third give out cricket-like twitters, it spreads to the strings, desk by desk through the winds and finally, as "the trill invades the world," to the full orchestra in a wide harmonic arc that finishes in E major, thus rounding off the monologue. (B 3.504)

In Toscanini's recording, Mariano Stabile fizzes and pings the consonants, rolls the liquids, punches the staccato vowels, in a way that makes the trill seem to boil straight from his blood into his voice. It is a wonder to hear the forward placement and glee of a phrase like *"e quivi risveglia il picciol fabbro dei trilli."* One can sense the fun Boito must have had in writing these sparkling lines. The deflated Falstaff has been reinflated.

But now comes Quickly, to begin the deflating all over again. This time she adds a new note to her invitation to meet Alice, one that involves risk and midnight and the supernatural. She describes the Black Hunter's haunting of the oak tree in a way that makes it a test of Falstaff's courage to venture there. He is being given some dignity in this outing—at least to begin with. Mistress Quickly tells the story of Herne, to spooky music, in a monotone as if hypnotized or hypnotizing:

By now, bassoons, horns and second violins have launched a chromatic *marche funèbre* with rapidly oscillating clarinet and low strings, and punctuated by timpany and bass and low, held brass chords. Gradually the harmonies thicken; yet the sound never rises above a pianissimo. (B 3.506)

This introduction of the supernatural takes us far away from the Marx Brothers shenanigans of the laundry basket, and sets

the scene for the astonishing last act, where Falstaff will in effect
be buried and raised again to life. Deflation will become a form
of sublimation.

Notes

1. James A. Hepokoski, *Giuseppe Verdi: Falstaff* (Cambridge University
   Press, 1983), p. 4.
2. Francis Toye, *Giuseppe Verdi: His Life and Works* (Vintage Books, 1959),
   p. 431.

15

Levitation

The opera has been earthy through the first two acts—pompously so with Falstaff, satirically so with the women. The last section in Act 3 lifts off from earth and becomes ethereal. The first sign of this is the love song of Fenton. For this Boito composed a sonnet, one with the Petrarchan rhyme scheme, not the Shakespearean. But this is both interrupted by the couplet already sung by Fenton and Nannetta (*"Bocca baciata . . ."*), and then suspended before the rhyme pattern can be completed, thus continuing the fleeting nature of the wooing in the earlier scenes. The song is one of long-distance yearning. It reaches out to a kiss never consummated. It is not a duet, but—until the last two lines—a monologue. The first quatrain drifts upward on *"lontano"* (far), and then falls softly back with the awaited response (*"parola"*):

> Dal labbro il canto estasiato vola
> Pei silenzi notturni e va lontano
> E alfin ritrova un altro labbro umano
> Che gli risponde colla sua parola.
> [Ecstatic song flies from the lips
> Through night's silence going far
> Until an answering voice
> Brings the responding song.]

The second quatrain quickens with new urgency, with soft staccato notes as dawn approaches and a voice responds. For the first time in the opera a harp is sounded, and a flutter of flutes and piccolo breathes through *"aer antelucano"* (air toward dawn):

> Allor la nota che non è più sola
> Vibra di gioia in un accordo arcano
> E innamorando l'aer antelucano
> Con altra voce al suo fonte rivola.
> [The tune, now no longer alone,
> Thrills secret in another breast,
> And amorous air, toward dawn,
> Carries a new voice singing back.]

The interrupted sestet tries to consummate the kiss, but only at a distance:

> Quivi ripiglia suon, ma la sua cura
> Tende sempre ad unir chi lo disuna.
> Così baciai la disiata bocca!
> Bocca baciata non perde ventura . . .
> . . . Anzi rinnova come fa la luna.
> [Here the song, replying, strains
> To join what it responds to.
> So I kissed the far-off lips.
> Lips kissed lose not what is to come . . .
> . . . They re-arise, a returning moon.]

Alice breaks off the song, to prepare for Falstaff's arrival at the oak. Fenton's aria is the exception that proves this opera's antiformalistic rule. Joseph Kerman sees how it fits in:

In *Falstaff* Verdi nearly completed his campaign against the aria, the most venerable symbol of opera's formality and artificiality. The title character is given no aria, only a diminutive canzonetta (which has proved susceptible, however, to encores); Ford gets a dramatic monologue; Mistress Quickly, a brief, free solo number; and Nannetta in her disguise as the Queen of Fairies, a song with chorus. Only Fenton, the tenor, gets an actual aria, a gift-offering to the opera audience, and also a wry acknowledgment that his voice then as now is the one irrevocably marked operatic. As to artifice, Fenton's aria is set to a sonnet. And lest these little jokes, among so many in *Falstaff*, seem too esoteric, Fenton is made to relinquish the end of his aria to Nannetta, and when he tries to recoup by singing along with her, the two of them are unceremoniously cut short by Alice, the operatic (or, rather, anti-operatic) Mistress Ford.[1]

Falstaff strides into this night scene wearing the antlers of Herne the Hunter. Then, suddenly timorous, he counts off the twelve strokes of midnight. His own notes do not vary, but each pulse is given a new harmonic note of mystery, what Toye calls "heart-searching harmonies."[2] Falstaff invokes Jove, who became a bull to woo Europa. When Alice shivers that Meg is coming, Falstaff revels in the thought of a threesome: "Dismember me [*squartatemi*], shred me [*sbranatemi*], as your shared meal of game meat." But Meg screams, "The witches are here!" and she and Alice run away. Falstaff recoils, and hears Nannetta singing as the fairy queen, summoning nymphs, elves, sylphs, and sirens: "The enchanting star rises," she proclaims. The choir of children answers her, and Falstaff throws himself on the ground, saying,

"These are the Fates. Seeing them is death." Nannetta now leads the choir in ravishing fairy music, the kind of music Mendelssohn will give Titania and her attendants in *A Midsummer Night's Dream*. Boito is drawing on that play here, more even than on *Merry Wives*.

But then the plotters come on in outlandish goblin disguises. Directors let their imaginations go wild here, conjuring up monsters and ogres from Bosch paintings. It was noticed earlier that people try to find a parallel for Jago's "Credo" in the Mefistofele of Boito's own opera. I think it would be fairer to say that Boito, when writing the grotesqueries of this scene, was remembering his witches' sabbath from *Mefistofele*. As the witches and warlocks (*streghe e stregoni*) in that scene punch out their witch-sabbath cry (*Saboè*) like lashes over Faust, he sees the specter of Margherita and repents what he has done to her.

Verdi's *Macbeth* was criticized for not equaling the spookiness of Weber's Wolf's Glen scene. But Bernard Shaw, it will be remembered, found that scene inadvertently comic. It can be said that Verdi has created in *Falstaff* a scene advertently comic, a spoof of the spooky, and Boito gave him the weird text for doing it. The Halloween versions of Bardolfo and Pistola order Falstaff to get up. He says he'll need a crane (*grue*) to lift him. He stays stretched on his stomach. This scene is going to end with forgiveness all around, and Boito has in mind the greatest predecessor for such a general amnesty, the end of *Le Nozze di Figaro*. In that opera's conclusion, the Count says that love "pricks at me, stabs at me" (*Mi pizzica, mi stuzzica*). Boito had that in mind when he gave the "elves" their chant as they punish the prone Falstaff:

Pizzica, pizzica,
Pizzica, stuzzica,

Levitation

Spizzica, spizzica,
Pungi, spiluzzica
Finch'egli abbài.
[Prick-at-him, prick-at-him
Prick-at-him, stab-at-him,
Poke-at-him, poke-at-him
Puncture-him, scrape-at-him,
Work till he howls.]

Alice, Meg, and Quickly now join the children in their chant:

Cozzalo, aizzalo
Dai piè al cocuzzolo
Strozzalo, strizzalo,
Gli svampi l'uzzolo.
Pizzica, pizzica, l'unghia rintuzzola
Ruzzola, ruzzola, ruzzola, ruzzola.
[Pound-on-him, prod-at-him
From noggin to foot of him,
Choke-at-him, squash-at-him,
Prick-at-him, prick-at-him,
Blot out the brain-of-him,
Prick-at-him, prick-at-him, tear at his nails,
Toss-him-round, toss-him-round, toss-him-round,
        toss-him-round.]

The plotters now hurl execrations at Falstaff, calling on him to repent all his sins. He howls, in a litany, *"Ahi! Ahi!, mi pento,"* becoming as penitent as Bardolfo and Pistola had been at the beginning of Act 2. When his accusers get more specific, Falstaff responds with a pun. They are invoking the Lord (*Domine*) against him, and he begs for salvation indeed—but means that they should save his belly (*addomine*):

> Domine fallo casto.
>   Ma salvagli l'addomine.
> [Make him chaste, my Lord.
>   My lard, keep *it* safe.]

The abjuring of the devil and all his ways was part of the baptismal ceremony, which was also a form of exorcism. And that is what this ceremonial scene has become. The most effective staging of it I know is a DVD of the 1976 Glyndebourne production by Jean-Pierre Ponnelle, with Donald Gramm as Falstaff and John Pritchard conducting. During the chant of "save him, Lord," the exorcism takes a solemn form—Falstaff is lifted up and carried supine in procession by ecclesiastical men. Then, at the end of the litany, as further accusations end in repeated demands (*"Rispondi"*), he is actually tossed in the air, as if aerating him from diabolic infection. This is indeed "making light of the man." One wonders if a singer heavier than Gramm could be treated this way (though his porters were obviously big men themselves). The pangs of a spiritual parturition are vividly enacted here—and that is the point of an exorcism/baptism: that a man be given a new birth.

When Falstaff recognizes Bardolfo and looses a stream of invective on him, he seems to revert to his old bullying relationship with the man, but his recognition of Ford leads Alice to reveal that he is her husband. Mistress Quickly shows her hand with a *"Cavalier-EHR-o."* Reality catches up with Falstaff.

To donkey-braying in the orchestra he admits: "It begins to dawn on me that I was a jackass."

But when all laugh at him, the man who did not lose all his dignity even in the Thames comes forward and claims to be the source of the vital energy around him, even that used against him: "I see the cheaper sort deride me. But, I absent, where would be the spice to this tale? For I, even I, am the point of it all. My first wink makes all the rest wink." And the rest all cry "Bravo!"—as Bardolfo and Pistola had cried *"Falstaff immenso! Enorme Falstaff!"* in Act I.

After Falstaff accepts his role as fool, Ford reveals his own folly, not only in his jealousy but in his opposition to his daughter's marriage to Fenton. And Doctor Cajus sees that he foolishly married the masked Bardolfo. As in the famous cartoon by Thomas Nast, everyone ends up pointing at everyone:

FALSTAFF: Who is the laughingstock?
FORD (indicating Cajus): He.
CAJUS (indicating Ford): You.
FORD: No.
CAJUS: Yes.
BARDOLFO (indicating Ford and Caius): Both.
FENTON: Both.
CAJUS (with Ford): We.
FALSTAFF: The batch of two. [*Tutti e due.*]
ALICE: No. The batch of three. [*No. Tutti e tre.*]

All the fools are out now and laughed at—and laughing. And forgiving one another. As Falstaff leads off the fugue, its point is made in roundabout canonic interweavings of the whole company's insight:

> Tutti gabbàti! Irride
> L'un l'altro ogni mortal.
> Ma ride ben chi ride
> La risata final.
> [All fall to con men. Every mortal
> Laughs at every other.
> But the best laugh is that
> Which is laughed last.]

Most commentators, like Budden (3.530), think there is a reference here to Shakespeare's *As You Like It* (2.7.139–40):

> All the world's a stage,
> And all the men and women merely players.

But Boito was drawing in this last scene on *A Midsummer Night's Dream,* and the obvious echo is of Puck's "Lord, what fools these mortals be!" (3.2.115). In any event, Boito managed to give the last word to Shakespeare.

Notes

1. Joseph Kerman, "The Verdi Blues," *New Republic,* January 10, 1994.
2. Francis Toye, *Giuseppe Verdi: His Life and Works* (Vintage Books, 1959), p. 435.

Acknowledgments

Barbara Gaines, of the Chicago Shakespeare Theater, who has directed both *Macbeth* the play and *Macbeth* the opera, read the whole book and made valuable suggestions. Rudolph Weingartner, longtime member of the Pittsburgh Symphony board of directors and chair of its artistic committee, likewise read it all and contributed new ideas. Philip Gossett, the great musical scholar, gave me valuable advice in the early stages of this project. My editor, Carolyn Carlson, and my agent, Andrew Wylie, were invaluable.

Index

Index

Index

Index

Index

Index

Index

Index

Index

AVAILABLE FROM PENGUIN

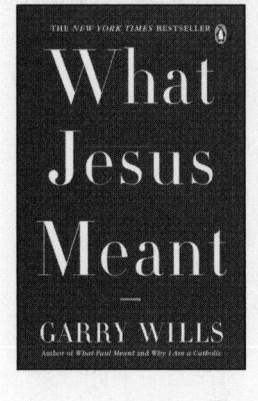 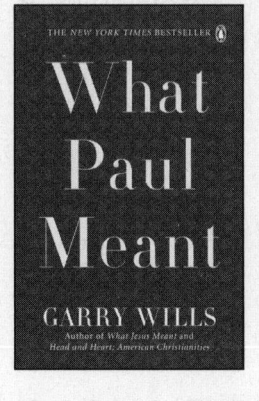 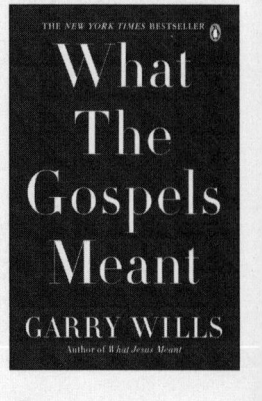

BY GARRY WILLS

PENGUIN BOOKS